“Grace Jacob welcor [illegible] other authors. Not only [illegible] of what missionary life is like inside Communist China, we discover through Grace’s transparency that missionaries are simply human—clay pots the Lord has graciously chosen to bring the excellency of the grace of Christ to others. But there is more. Grace offers us an account of her evangelistic encounters, not so that we might admire her courage or ability—quite the contrary—but so that, through them, we might discover a helpful approach to take in our relationships with those who do not yet know the Savior. I highly recommend you read *Faith Ride* for insight into missionary life and how to pray for missionaries, but also as a guidebook for your gospel proclamation.”

Rev. Doug McMasters
Senior Pastor, New Hyde Park Baptist Church, New Hyde Park, New York

“I enjoyed reading Grace Jacob’s brutally honest and faith-filled account of her family’s experiences over many years of ministry for Jesus Christ in Hong Kong and China … [*Faith Ride*] provides invaluable insights into life in China for anyone considering Christian service there.”

Paul Hattaway
Co-author of *The Heavenly Man*
Founder of Asia Harvest

“*Faith Ride* engages us in the powerful story of life-on-life mission work in Hong Kong and China. As the author and her family live out their faith before neighbors, friends and students, all kinds of challenges and adventures unfold. Skillfully weaved into the narrative is an apologetic for the Gospel, that can easily translate into the context of the reader. *Faith Ride* is a testament to the faithfulness of God and how He can work through a life fully devoted to serving Him.”

Rev. Brenden Bridges, MACL
Senior Pastor, Richvale Community Church, Richvale, California

“Jacob’s second book continues her contribution of compelling stories about her and her husband’s engagements for Christ in China. These days, we so need encouragement and inspiration to do the work of reaching out with the gospel to those without His hope, whatever our life context. The book takes the narratives, brings them alive, and provides application for each of us. Highly recommended."

John Townsend, Ph.D.
Psychologist and author of the New York Times bestselling *Boundaries* book series
Founder, Townsend Institute for Leadership and Counseling

"I was moved to tears of joy. How can you not be inspired watching the Holy Spirit move in the life of a willing servant as well as the lives of those he wants to redeem!"

Patrick T. Foutz
Pastor, Redemption Fellowship, Tukwila, Washington
President, Transform

"The stories in *Faith Ride* are amazing! They will strengthen your faith and open windows into the heart of God. Grace's love for China and its people shines throughout the book. Because of her openness about her failings as well as her successes, we clearly see God's faithfulness in every situation. The book ends with helpful insights about how to share Christ with our friends of other faiths, especially Buddhists."

Lois Dow, PhD
Professor Emerita, McMaster Divinity College
Missionary to Nigeria for 30 years

"Writing out of her own experience, Grace Jacob has produced a moving account of the work of God in the lives of her Chinese friends. Along the way, she paints a helpful picture of the challenges of transcultural evangelism in settings such as China. *Faith Ride* is not only a great ride, it's a great read."

Dr. Malcolm Brewer
Retired Pastor in the Seattle, Washington area

"This was a detailed and personal account of living out Christianity in raw, vivid life situations in a hostile environment. It was an exposé of Chinese culture, with compelling stories of faith, conflict, disappointments, and gospel outreach. It was a fascinating read."

Bob Higgins
Founder of Otino Waa Children's Village, Uganda
Former missionary to Uganda

"If you have ever wondered what it's like to do gospel work in the hardest of places, *Faith Ride* is an insider's story that is compelling and convicting for the Christian."

Jody Faison
Community Pastor, Eastmont Church, Bend, Oregon

FAITH RIDE

True Adventures of Faith and Evangelism from China

Grace Jacob

Bend, Oregon

Faith Ride: True Adventures of Faith and Evangelism from China

Printed in the United States of America

ISBN 978-0-692-87921-4

Editing by Jerri Menges Editing

Cover design by Faceout Studio, (Tim Green), www.faceoutstudio.com

This book is dedicated to Hanni Planos

Hanni was on the missions committee of one of our supporting churches.
In Mainland China,
I would not have made it through everything we faced
and I could not have served the Lord there
without Hanni's frequent phone calls, encouragement, support, and prayers.
She always believed in me,
and we both opened our hearts to each other.
I suspect that on Judgment Day, when I stand before the Lord,
Hanni will be standing next to me,
and I believe that any well done the Lord tells me for any work I have done,
he will tell her the same well done for the same work.
Matthew 10:41-42

AUTHOR'S NOTE

The stories in *Faith Ride* are true. I have recreated events, locales, and conversations to the best of my memory. I also referred to my notes, letters, and photographs, and I asked others who were present.

To protect our Chinese friends, the names of most individuals—including my name and the names of my husband and sons—and the names of most cities in Mainland China are pseudonyms. On rare occasions inconsequential details or identifying characteristics have been changed.

Most of the conversations took place in Cantonese or Mandarin. The translations are mine.

INTRODUCTION

"...those who hope in the Lord will renew their strength.
They will soar on wings like eagles; they will run and not grow weary,
they will walk and not be faint."
Isaiah 40:31

When I was 30 and my husband was 33, at the calling of the Lord, we packed up our two sons, ages three and one, and flew 18 hours to hot, humid, muggy Hong Kong. The first thing we did was learn the ancient, monosyllabic, seven-toned language of Hong Kong, Cantonese, which was a bear to learn and a joy to speak. Cantonese is the most beautiful, emotional, and expressive language I know. And it naturally lends itself to humor.

The Westerners I met who toured Hong Kong only took in the tall, architecturally handsome skyscrapers of Hong Kong Island and Tsim Sha Tsui on the Kowloon peninsula. They would tell me, "This is just like New York City." But they didn't know the back alleys, the villages, the ancient culture, and the people's passions and pride that we came to know. The visitors couldn't see that culturally Hong Kong is one of the most Chinese places in the world.

While living in Hong Kong, Chinese festivals became the way our family marked off the seasons of the year, celebrating each one to its fullest with specialty foods, colorful decorations, and historically or mythically based activities rich with meaning. When we moved to Mainland China, we came to realize that the Chinese there knew little of their own Chinese festivals because communism had set out to obliterate the culture. We taught our new Mainland Chinese friends how to celebrate each festival—what to eat and its significance, what to hang on their windows and doors, what activities to enjoy as a family, and what the stories behind each celebration were.

In Mainland China, we learned Mandarin in order to be able to work, shop, enjoy deep friendships, share the gospel, and teach the Bible. In the Mainland, Cantonese became our secret family language that we used to tell confidences and express our wilder emotions.

§§§

I was never the best person to share the gospel, but I was usually the only person. Many of my friends didn't know another Christian. Furthermore, because communist China was such a low-trust society, some of my Mainland Chinese friends didn't trust other Chinese people, but, amazingly, they trusted me, a foreigner. I was even told by one Chinese friend that if another Chinese person had told her about Jesus, she would not have believed it.

Although I had a few halting successes in sharing the gospel in Hong Kong, it was in Mainland China that I developed my understanding of how to share about Jesus—how to step into the shoes of my friends and explain the gospel from their perspectives, how to ask questions, how to use a parallel example to get across a point ... I will forever be grateful to the Lord for teaching me these methods because many of my Chinese friends I will see again when we are finally with the Lord. One of my Chinese friends has repeatedly messaged me from China about how excited she is that the two of us will be reunited in heaven and how we will worship the Lord together. I also can't wait to be with my Chinese friends again when we see the Lord. I want to dance with them with all our might in an attempt to give the Lord the glory due his name.

§§§

Recently I was talking with a woman who had just finished reading my previous book, *Dragon Ride*. She said to me, "You had to have been a woman of great faith to be able to go through everything you faced and to serve the Lord the way you did." I told her, "No, not at all! You have it completely backward—you got cause and effect mixed up. I didn't have a lot of faith when I went into those trials; it was *because of* all those trials that my faith grew. I had to learn to trust the Lord with each new trial or I would have gone under."

Living by faith felt like a wild ride.

Every time my husband and I faced a new insurmountable problem, we got really scared. These were life-threatening, kid-destroying, career-ending, poverty-inflicting problems. The two of us would sit down in the living room and recount all the previous impossible situations the Lord had brought us through. By the time we finished, we knew the Lord would see us through this current problem as well. That's how faith grows, by being plunged into trials with the Lord. And that's how the Lord shows his fatherly love for us, by training us through the trials he's submersed us in (Hebrews 12:5-11).

In China I used to tell my husband that I always felt like I was walking on the edge of a knife. Any false step and I would fall off and be destroyed. Then I came to realize that the Lord was holding the knife. Anytime I was about to tumble off, he shifted it to keep me from falling. But some of my imminent crashes would have been so momentous that moving the knife wouldn't have saved me. Then it dawned on me that the Lord's other hand was under the knife to catch me when shifting the knife wouldn't have been enough. Realizing that calmed me down. Living by faith in the Lord is the safest place to be. I am always secure in the Lord's hands, no matter how dangerous my circumstances or my failings.

The calling the Lord placed on me and my family to be missionaries in Hong Kong and China, I wouldn't have exchanged for the world. It stretched me, broke me, humbled me, broadened my views, deepened my relationship with the Lord, opened my eyes to the relevance of the Scriptures, and taught me to pray fervently and lean on the Lord in faith. And I learned to share the gospel in Asia. I loved the Chinese friends I made, and they loved me. I would go back in a flash to see them and live in China again if I could. Every fiber of my soul aches to be in China, palling around with my Chinese friends there.

My family and I have walked with the Lord for many exciting years. Come join us on this ride of faith!

LIST OF STORIES

BRIEF BACKGROUND AND HONG KONG
1986-1995

MAINLAND CHINA
1996-2015

BONUS
A GOD BEYOND COMPARISON

JESUS, THE SORCERER?

1999-2000, Wuran

This was my first attempt at doing something like this. We had only been living in Mainland China for three years when I invited two college students I had never met to my home, hoping it would lead to us studying the Bible together.

Pedaling my clunky, black Flying Pigeon bike as fast as it would go, I tried to make up for lost time as I raced the mile and a half from my home to the university where I was to meet them. Explaining how to find my apartment had been too complicated, so we agreed to meet at the west gate of the university.

The pollution-tinted orange ball of the August sun was sinking toward the horizon when I arrived. The wide iron gate, set way back from the road, left a yawning space crowded with students milling about. I dismounted and wiped my sweaty brow.

Since this was before the age of cell phones in China, I scanned the students' faces to see if anyone paid attention to me—that would be my signal. I only knew the couple's chosen English names: Nate and Kathy.

A tall young man, holding hands with a much shorter woman, smiled and nodded at me; he was walking a "dating bike"—a standard bike with a back-wheel axle extender for the girlfriend to stand on.

Just as I started to walk over to them, I noticed a middle-aged guard in gray uniform on the left side of the gate staring intently at me. He frowned, then speed-walked in my direction while glancing at the couple. I hadn't expected interference from a guard, but then we were in the middle of one of the Chinese government's many crackdowns on Christianity.

Immediately I signaled to the couple by shifting my eyes and tilting my head slightly to the right to tell them to follow me. I was hoping they caught my meaning, but that the movement was so subtle the guard wouldn't see it.

In that split second I saw confusion on the face of the young man, but I had to get away before the guard reached me, so I jumped on my bike and raced away without looking back. Fortunately, the couple understood my signal and biked after me before the guard was able to catch up with them either.

Only after we entered the safety of my apartment and shut the door behind us did I see them clearly. Nate's angular jaw gave him a distinguished look. His eyes were a little pensive, even as he smiled his open, friendly smile. I liked him immediately—he had a face I could trust. He reached out his hand and greeted me with a warm handshake.

Kathy, his girlfriend, was beautiful, her hair cut just below her shoulders. But her oval face was cloaked and her smile tentative, as if she were concealing something, and her eyes didn't smile with her lips.

Neither of them spoke much English.

I had gotten connected with Nate through a team of Australian Christian college students, whom my husband, Justin, had arranged to study in our city for two weeks. Just before they returned to Australia, they told Justin they had led Nate to the Lord and gave Justin Nate's number. So I cold-called Nate, mentioned that I knew the Australians, and invited him to my home. He asked if he could bring his girlfriend.

After we sat down in my living room, I offered Nate and Kathy sodas. "Do you know why I biked away and didn't wait for you?" I asked in Mandarin, feeling awkward.

"We have no idea," Nate said.

I told them about the guard and a little about the security issues in

China, but they didn't understand. Most of the unbelievers we knew in Mainland China had no idea that their government persecutes Christians. I didn't say much to Nate and Kathy because I didn't want to scare them off.

Then we talked about their college majors, their families, the Australian students, and Nate's decision to follow Christ. Finally I asked, "Would you like to study the Bible together?"

They looked at each other, and I could see excitement in their faces. Nate turned to me and said, "We'd love to."

We decided to meet once a week. I told them, "On the phone we shouldn't mention studying the Bible; we'll speak in code—even though we'll be studying in Mandarin, we'll refer to what we're doing as studying English."

Before we met again, I prayed and prepared a lot. I had only just finished three years of studying Mandarin and this was the first time I was going to lead a Bible study *in Mandarin*. I was quite nervous, and as it turned out I had a lot of reason to be nervous.

The next week I brought them up to the second floor of our apartment to a room with a lot of character—the warm chestnut vaulted ceiling angled right to the floor. Nate gently touched Kathy's shoulder to guide her to one of the chairs I had set up in a circle. After Nate sat down, Kathy leaned her knee against his.

Before we started studying the Bible, I told them how much I love the Lord and what he's done for me. They were very attentive. Then I explained that God is our creator, and I told them why Jesus had died for us on the cross. I wanted to make sure they were clear on the basics, and as far as I could tell, they both understood.

Then I handed them Chinese Bibles. They could hardly contain their excitement as they looked inside. They looked just the way I feel whenever I open my Bible. It turns out they had never seen a Bible before.

On that first day, we read the story of Jesus feeding the 5,000 so they could see Jesus' concern for our practical needs and his creative power. I didn't fully realize at that point how hard it is for Mainland Chinese people to understand Jesus' miracles.

After reading the story, both of them, but especially Kathy, looked puzzled for a few minutes. Finally she asked, "How could Jesus have fed so many people with so little food?"

She looked off in the distance for a moment, then her face suddenly brightened. "*Oh, I get it. Jesus is a sorcerer! He used sorcery to make the food.*"

Since I had studied Mandarin at a *government university*, I could speak fluently about general life, and current events, but, because China is officially an atheist country, we hadn't studied *any* religious vocabulary, and I had never heard the Chinese word for *sorcery*. So I didn't actually understand what Kathy said, but I thought I did. Since Jesus had performed a miracle, I guessed she was saying the word for *miracle*, so I smiled and agreed, and used the word she had used. What I thought I said in response was, "Yes, Jesus was performing a *miracle*. Isn't he powerful!" But what I actually said was, "Yes, Jesus was performing *black magic*. Isn't he powerful!"

Both of them agreed. Jesus was a great sorcerer.

Something bothered me about the interaction, though, so after they left, I looked up the word Kathy had used in my Chinese dictionary. I gasped when I saw it meant sorcery and realized I had agreed with Kathy that Jesus had used witchcraft to feed the 5,000! Ach!

Both Nate and Kathy had grown up as Buddhists. One time my husband and I had accidentally attended a Buddhist magical performance so I was a little familiar with Buddhist magic. Buddhism, with its magical power displays, had made it difficult for them to understand what a true miracle is. When Jesus fed the 5,000, it was a type of creation miracle, performed by the creator God. It wasn't black magic.

But Nate had supposedly committed his life to Christ. I was beginning to wonder who he thought he had committed his life to—a sorcerer?

After realizing my blunder, I also looked up the Chinese word for *miracle*. The next week I told them that Jesus was not a black magician; rather, he had performed a miracle.

"Miracle?" Nate asked, looking confused. "What's that? I've never heard that Chinese word before." Since the concept of a Christian miracle had been all but obliterated from the Chinese vocabulary by the atheist communist government, few people had heard the word *miracle*. I tried to explain, but with their limited exposure to the concept of a creator God who can perform miracles, I had little success. The atheism of their culture was blinding them.

Soon after that fiasco, we started studying the Gospel of John. Again we ran into problems, and right at the first verse! The standard Chinese Bible translation for John 1:1 is this: "In the beginning was the *dao*, and the *dao* was with God, and the *dao* was God." That *dao* means "way or path," but it's also the *dao* of Daoism (also called Taoism)![1]

Nate and Kathy were trying so hard to understand who the Christian God is, but the more I explained the verse, the more confused they became. They thought I was saying that the *dao* of Daoism was God! At first I didn't realize what the problem was, but after it dawned on me, I tried to backtrack. Finally the only thing I could do was move on and pretend that I hadn't told them that the *dao* was God. I hoped they'd forget.

This time it was Chinese Daoism, which pervades the culture, that had made God incomprehensible to them.

Had Nate actually become a Christian? I asked them why they wanted to study the Bible with me.

"We're curious about Christianity," Nate replied.

"That's it?" My heart sank.

"We're excited to be learning about Christianity," Kathy added.

"But, Nate," I said, "I thought you decided to commit your life to Christ."

Nate smiled. "The Australian college students were real nice, and I wanted to learn about Christianity, so when they asked if I wanted to follow Jesus, I agreed. All I meant was that I was curious about Christianity."

That was such a typical problem with the Mainland Chinese—if they like you and want to honor you, many will readily agree when you ask if they want to believe in Jesus. But they may not mean anything by

---

[1] The Greek word *logos* is packed with meaning. Translating it as "word" in Chinese makes even less sense than it does in English. In order to make the Chinese translation comprehensible, the translator probably borrowed "way" from John 14:6 "I am the way (*dao*) ..."

it.

I was so disappointed—Nate hadn't come to faith yet. Another botch! I wasn't discipling Nate; neither of them knew Christ.

We needed to go back to the basics. So, again, I started with who God is. And you know what Nate said? "We love learning about the Christian way of reaching the Christian god in the Christian heaven! Since we're Buddhists, all we've ever heard about was the Buddhist way of reaching the Buddhist god in the Buddhist heaven, nirvana."

I was stunned. I had been working under the assumption that when we talked about God, we were talking about the same entity. We were not on the same page at all!

Furthermore, in their thinking, Buddhism and Christianity were equally valid and true, but completely different. I felt like I was way over my head. I tried to deal with the concept of only one way to God the only way I knew how. Opening to John 14:6 in my Chinese Bible, I read, "Jesus answered, 'I am the way and the truth and the life. No one comes to the Father except through me.'"

Kathy looked disappointed. "Of course the Bible would say that because it wants people to only believe in Jesus!"

I sighed. The cool winds of mid-October were already blowing by this time. I had been praying for this couple and our Bible study all along, but after that session I spent a lot of time on my knees, asking the Lord to give me insight to get through this impasse. The Lord had to reveal himself to them (Matthew 11:27), and he needed to give me spiritual wisdom to get through to them (I Corinthians 2:13).

The next month there was quite a turnaround in their thinking.

Nate began one of the sessions by telling me, "We've been talking about this a lot. Both of us really want to become Christians because we can see that the Christian God is so good. We want to believe, but there's something stopping us, and we don't know what it is."

So I asked them to write out all their questions to help me figure out what was blocking them from believing.

From our discussions and reading their questions, I got the impression they thought that the Christian God had created the Christians and the Buddhist god had created the Buddhists. Sort of like parallel religious universes. And it was clear they didn't believe in absolute truth. So again I talked about the fact that there is only one true God, the Christian God, and he created *everything*. But this time I emphasized that he created *all people*, even Buddhists. I could see this was a new concept for them, but something clicked in their understanding, so I felt we could move on.

Then we talked about sin, that it is God who decides what's right and wrong, not us, and how sin is an offense to God. It took a while, but they began to understand.

The next week I told them that God has a standard by which we are to live.

Nate was appalled. "Whoa! I don't like the idea of God having laws for me to follow. I can't agree with somebody telling me what to do just because he wants to!"

Kathy joined in. "Yeah, that's not right! Even though he's our creator! He might just have his own agenda for wanting us to obey his laws. We don't want to follow the Christian God if he's like that!"

I showed them Isaiah 48:17-18. "I am the Lord your God, who teaches you what is best for you, who directs you in the way you should go. If only you had paid attention to my commands, your peace would have been like a river, your well-being like the waves of the sea."

Kathy calmed down. "Oh, I see. God knows what's best for us because he created us, and he gave us these laws because they're good for us!"

After that we talked about God's purity and more about his goodness, and how no one who is sinful can get near to God. I could see that the more I talked about God's goodness, the more they truly were attracted to him. They began to smile more, and Nate was leaning forward, intent on everything I had to say. I again brought up the death of Jesus on the cross and told them that Jesus had died in our place to take the punishment for our sins. If we put our sins on Jesus' cross and turn away from them, we can receive forgiveness, be pure, and come close to God.

For a few weeks now, whenever I brought up God, they only thought about the Christian God, not the Buddhist god or any other god. But they still didn't really understand that the only way to come to God is through Jesus. Finally it dawned on me that I could use the

Buddhist concept of more than one way to god to make the truth of the gospel clear to them.

I formed a fist with my left hand and held it up to represent God. Holding my right hand about a foot away, I pointed my right index finger at my fist and slowly moved it along a path until it touched my fist. "*This* is the Buddhist way to God," I said.

Then I moved my right hand to a different spot, indicating a different path, and again pointed my index finger at my fist and moved my hand along the new path toward my fist. "*This* is the Christian way to get to God."

They both nodded.

Then, indicating yet a different path, I moved my right hand to another starting point and made the same motion toward my fist and said, "And *this* is the Muslim path to reach God. Is that about right—each religion has its own path?"

They both nodded again.

Then I asked, "Since everyone, including Buddhists, has sinned, and since as sinners we can't come close to God because he's so good and pure, how does *anyone*, including a Buddhist, get rid of his sin in order to get close to God?"

Kathy pondered this for a few minutes. Then suddenly she had an aha moment, "Since Jesus is the only one who can forgive sins, everyone would have to come through him! There's no other way. *Even Buddhists need Jesus to get to God!*" She looked at Nate, her face flushed. She had discovered for herself that Jesus is the only way.

There are many paths to God, but because we're sinful only one of them works.

I asked if they wanted to come to God through Jesus. Nate said he wanted to. He prayed very slowly, his voice cracking with emotion. Then he began to cry. "As you've been talking about God, Grace, I really wanted to believe in him, but something was blocking me. Now the obstacle is gone! I truly believe in him now."

Then Kathy prayed, confessing her sins and committing her life to Christ. She wasn't as emotional as Nate, but joy filled her face as she looked up. She had found her heart's desire.

How had this happened when I was so eminently incapable?

The next time we met they couldn't wait to tell me how everything had changed now that they believed in Jesus. With a twinkle in his eye, Nate summed it up, "It's so different when you aren't controlling your own life."

Kathy, especially, started reading the Bible a lot on her own. When they came over, she told me, "I came across a verse that says sin is disobeying what God tells us to do." Her eyes widened. "I've got to finish reading the Bible quickly so I'll know everything God tells us to do! I don't want to sin."

A few weeks later I told them about Jesus coming back again. Kathy looked upset. "But I don't know if I'll recognize him when he returns!"

I showed them Matthew 24:26-27, 30, "So if anyone tells you, 'There he is, out in the wilderness,' do not go out; or, 'Here he is, in the inner rooms,' do not believe it. For as lightning that comes from the east is visible even in the west, so will be the coming of the Son of Man ... when they see the Son of Man coming on the clouds of heaven, with power and great glory."

Nate chuckled. He looked lovingly over at Kathy and said, "Kathy, if you don't know if it's Jesus or not, then it's not Jesus!"

Starting from the first week after they came to know the Lord, both of them were sharing Christ with a lot of their friends.

One day Kathy came over looking upset. "Some of my closest friends told me that I was duped into believing Christianity. That really hurts. They've been criticizing me and laughing at me. They told me that everything in the Bible is too incredible—it can't have happened. I told them, '*If you know the power of God, it's not unbelievable at all!*' But sometimes one of my friends does show an interest in Jesus, and then I buy a Bible for her." In just a few weeks this couple had grown to love the Lord to the point that they were willing to suffer humiliation for Jesus as they shared him with their friends.

The Lord had broken through all their false belief systems and spiritual blindness. For my part, I had to find out what was blocking them from understanding the gospel, then step into their shoes and start from their starting point in order to explain the gospel from their perspective.

BRIEF BACKGROUND AND HONG KONG

1986-1995

My first book, *Dragon Ride*,
told the story of how I came to know Jesus,
and how I met Justin, my husband,
while we were each studying for our Master of Divinity degree
at Trinity Evangelical Divinity School.
We were married in our Chinese church in 1982.
The Lord had called Justin to become a missionary
to the Chinese people in Asia.

First, as a couple, we planted a church for Cambodian refugees
near Seattle, Washington.
While in the Seattle area, I gave birth to two sons,
Nigel and Adam.

Our mission agency then sent us to Hong Kong as church
planters.
Nigel was three and Adam, one,
when we embarked on this adventure.

In Hong Kong
Justin and I studied Cantonese full-time for the first two years
and part-time with a tutor for our third year.
After that we planted two Cantonese churches.

Justin was fulfilling the dream the Lord had placed in his heart
and I was passionate about evangelism.

ANTICIPATION

1986-1990, Hong Kong

"Justin, look out the window! Are we gonna crash into the buildings?"

The plane was flying so low I could see women hanging laundry on the rooftops. I pulled our two young sons close.

A few years before, Justin had flown into Hong Kong just over the tops of the apartment buildings, so he wasn't too worried. But I had never even visited Hong Kong and had never imagined such a descent. And it was dangerous—Kai Tak Airport, located in densely populated Kowloon, was one of the most dangerous airports in the world.[2] But we finally did land safely on the tarmac.

Justin and I were in our early 30s and were moving to Hong Kong with our three- and one-year-old sons, Nigel and Adam, to plant Cantonese churches. We couldn't wait to settle down in this crowded city, learn the language, make Chinese friends, and adjust to their culture. We hoped all four of us would become fluent so we could plant the churches together as a family.

As soon as our plane taxied to a stop and the doors opened, I

---

[2] https://www.travelchinaguide.com/cityguides/hongkong-kai-tak-airport.htm

breathed in my first breath of Hong Kong air. Ugh! It smelled like a sewer! The airport was at the edge of Victoria Harbor, and I later learned that terrible smell was the stench of that beautiful harbor.[3]

Justin and I, each schlepping four heavy carry-ons, tried to corral our boys down the aisle of the plane. When we finally made it to the door, I reeled back as I was hit with the most oppressive heat and humidity I had ever felt. *This smelly place with this horrible climate is where we're going to live?* It was a June night and even at night Hong Kong was still this hot and muggy! I could feel my excitement draining away.

When we reached the Arrivals Hall, we spotted several members of the Mission Personnel Committee who had come to welcome us, but within minutes our dream of integrating into Chinese culture came crashing down. "The mission has rented a great apartment for you!" one of them told us, beaming. "It's an apartment any missionary would love. It's on a hill overlooking the town of Tai Wai, and all your neighbors are American and British."

Justin and I looked at each other aghast. We didn't want to live in a foreign enclave. How were our kids supposed to learn Cantonese when they would be surrounded by English speakers?

It didn't take long for us to find out that there was a whole generation of missionary kids who didn't speak Chinese. The model was that the husband went off and did the missionary work in the local language, while the wife and kids went the English route and had no Cantonese ministry.

I was feeling more and more disillusioned. Isolation and separation wasn't the model we wanted for our family. And the way I'm built, I knew I'd probably be very unhappy if I ended up so insulated from the Chinese.

So within a few days, through a translator, we hired a sweet, freckled Chinese woman, Mrs. Mak, to babysit the kids every weekday morning while Justin and I studied the language at Chinese University. She didn't speak any English, so the boys would be immersed in

---

[3] The People's Republic of China made one great improvement in Hong Kong after Britain turned it over to them—they cleaned up Victoria Harbor.

Cantonese all morning, even though, for the time being, we would have to live surrounded by foreigners.

We thought it would be hard on our toddlers not to be able to communicate with their babysitter, but, like everything else in life, they saw it as an opportunity. They could take advantage of the babysitter any way they wanted since she couldn't tell them what to do. So on the first day of class, we got a call from the translator telling us the boys had dumped every shoe they could find into the fish tank and killed all the fish Mrs. Mak had given them as a gift. Could this arrangement even work when the babysitter had to call a translator just to keep order?

But Mrs. Mak loved our boys, and she often took them out for dim sum[4] while we were at school. Everyone in the restaurant wanted to touch their blond hair since it was such a novelty, but Mrs. Mak didn't like it. The AIDS epidemic had recently started in America, and Hong Kong people didn't seem to know how it was contracted; they just thought of it as an American disease. So with a straight face, Mrs. Mak stared down any violator reaching out their hand to touch the boys' hair, and said sternly, "He has AIDS!" The hand was immediately withdrawn and the violator ran back to his own table.

From spending every morning with Mrs. Mak, Nigel and Adam began to speak a little Cantonese. Children usually pick up languages easily, but Cantonese, with its seven tones, is such a difficult language that even kids find it hard to learn if their parents aren't native speakers.

When Nigel was four and a half, we decided to enroll him in Chinese kindergarten, naively thinking it would help his language acquisition. But it turned out the cultural and language adjustments were too difficult for Nigel. We noticed the first indication of a problem a month after he entered kindergarten, and it scared us.

Our American neighbors, who had two kids just older than ours, invited our family over for barbeque chicken and salads. We met on their porch, at the back of our apartment building on the sloping hillside, edged by tropical trees.

Nigel was normally a gregarious boy with a great sense of humor. But that day, when he walked onto the neighbors' porch, he only said

[4] Dim sum is a Cantonese breakfast of small pastries, dumplings, and delicacies.

"Hi," then stood with his back to the wall, refusing to speak a word to kids or adults for the rest of the afternoon. No matter how many toys, games or funny stories our neighbors tempted him with, he just stood there mute.

His straight blond hair framed his face, which had become a closed mask, his azure blue eyes clouded over. He was tense. Inscrutable. Determined.

I couldn't figure out why this sudden change of personality, so when we returned home, I asked him why he had been so silent at the barbeque.

He announced, "I will speak English only with you three inside our home. I will say 'hello' and 'thank you' to other English speakers, but I will say nothing else to them. And I will not speak Cantonese to anyone under any circumstances."

"Why, Nigel?"

"I don't know. But that is what I have decided."

Years later, I read about what we were seeing—selective mutism—"an anxiety disorder of childhood characterized by consistent failure to speak in specific social settings (as at school) despite having the ability to speak normally in other settings (as at home)."[5] But at the time we had no idea what was happening to our son.

And we didn't know what to do. Our son was in a lot of emotional pain and we were sure that it was because of the stress of speaking Cantonese at school that he had closed up into a protective cocoon. Here we were, trying to serve the Lord, and it was seriously harming our son.

At this point, all our hopes for ministry were crashing. If the kids didn't learn Cantonese, how were we going to be a church planting family? Just like the other missionaries, for church and ministry we'd have to split up—one of us parents, probably me, wouldn't be able to participate in the Chinese church plant and would have to go to an English-speaking church for the sake of the kids. We started to understand the other missionary families, why only the husband had Cantonese ministry.

---

[5] https://www.merriam-webster.com/medical/selective%20mutism

However, our ministry seemed like the lesser issue at this point. We didn't have a clue how to help Nigel or how to get him to speak again. We didn't know if taking him out of the Chinese kindergarten would help or harm him. If we took him out, it would certainly harm any Chinese ministry I would have.

One day, after Justin and I prayed for wisdom, he sat still on the couch for a few minutes, pondering. Finally he said, "If we can just see some progress, no matter how small, then we'll leave him in the school. But if he either stays this way or gets worse, then we need to pull him out." I breathed a sigh of relief—we had a plan. I still didn't have much hope; it was just a course of action that made sense.

We continued to pray fervently that Nigel would start speaking again, and week by week he did make small increments of progress and was willing to speak a word or two of *English* to others, so we kept him in the school. Eventually he calmed down, and even started speaking a little Cantonese. Every time Nigel said a word in public, Justin and I silently cheered. No one around us knew how significant every single word was!

Later we found out why he developed the courage to speak. His Chinese kindergarten teacher had seen Nigel's struggle and was fighting for him. She told us, "I knew Nigel had potential and could speak Cantonese even though he was refusing to, so I made him my translator for the other American kid in the class—that way Nigel had to speak." Thank God for a sensitive, caring kindergarten teacher. She had no idea that her kindness and creativity hadn't just saved Nigel, it had also rescued our family's ministry in Hong Kong. The significance of a small kindness.

A year later, the four of us were walking through a park and Nigel was jabbering away to us in Cantonese when a Chinese woman ahead of us glanced back, then did a double take when she saw Nigel. "I thought it was a Chinese kid talking. I can't believe a white kid can speak Cantonese that fluently!"

The Lord had answered our prayers. It had been essential for us not to give up too quickly when we faced setbacks and hardships in doing the Lord's work.

By God's grace, the four of us, as a family, were able to plant two

Cantonese churches in Hong Kong. And the kids not only made lots of Chinese friends, they even led some of them to the Lord using Cantonese.

SEARCHING FOR COMMON GROUND

1988-1990 Hong Kong

After living almost two years in the secluded foreign enclave overlooking the town of Tai Wai, we were excited to finally move to our first Chinese village, Tin Sam Village. This laid-back village was located in the bustling heart of Tai Wai, in the New Territories. We noticed that when we entered the village, life slowed down. The streets were paved with gray cobblestone, and every apartment building was three stories high and two apartments wide, with white tile siding and red, glazed-tile roof. In spite of the uniformity, I found the village quaint.

Every few days an old man strolled through the village with a long pole over his shoulder. At the end of the pole was a wooden bucket full of fresh, soft, warm, dessert tofu (pronounced *dow fa*). All through the village, we could hear his loud, distinctive call, drawing out the low-toned "dow," then following it quickly with the high-pitched "fa!" As soon as our sons heard his call, they would run over to where I was, beg me for one Hong Kong dollar each, then grab bowls, and race out to join all the other kids in the village who were swarming around the tofu seller. The old man would unshoulder his pole, dish out steaming tofu into each child's bowl, and top it with warm sugarcane syrup. It was one of the many delights of Hong Kong, and the boys loved it; they were already fitting into Hong Kong life.

As for me, six months into our move, I was still an oddity in the village. Although the neighbors were kind, I hadn't succeeded in making any friends, and I was lonely. I kept noticing the Chan family who lived on the second floor across the cobblestone alley from us. None of them spoke any English. Every day after school, the two gangly pre-adolescent sons returned home with huge backpacks so heavy they had to lean way forward to carry them.

The mom especially interested me. Mrs. Chan was in her early 40s—about ten years my senior—with permed, curly hair cut in a blunt bob at her ears. Her face widened beautifully at her jaw, especially when she smiled at me. She wasn't lively or boisterous; she just calmly went about her business in the village, and it was only after becoming friends with her that I realized how beautiful she was inside. She was a salt-of-the-earth person—kind, honest, and refreshingly simple.

I believe the Lord laid her on my heart because he was planning to draw her to himself.

And I prayed fervently that we could become friends. But when we bumped into each other in the alley, our conversations never seemed to go deeper than the friendly Cantonese greetings. I would often look longingly up at her apartment, racking my brain for how to become friends with her. We weren't familiar enough with Hong Kong culture to know how the Chinese made friends. When the Mid-Autumn Festival arrived, I decided to give Mrs. Chan a tin of delicious lotus paste mooncakes,[6] the festival's celebration food, to see if that would start a friendship.

It worked, but almost too well. Immediately, Mrs. Chan adopted me as her friend. The next day, I was in the bathroom of our ground floor apartment helping Adam go to the potty when I heard the doorbell buzz. Since I wasn't free, I didn't go answer it. It buzzed and buzzed for a minute or two before going silent. Then I heard Mrs. Chan call to me in Cantonese through my living room window, "Mrs. Jeung,

---

[6] Mooncakes are special small cakes filled with seed or bean paste and a preserved egg yolk to represent the moon.

Mrs. Jeung,[7] are you home?" Next, I heard her at Justin's and my bedroom window calling, then at the boys' bedroom window, "Mrs. Jeung, Mrs. Jeung! Where are you?" Finally, through the translucent privacy film on the bathroom window, I saw the darkened shape of her head with her hand leaning against the window above her face, shading her eyes. "Mrs. Jeung, Mrs. Jeung! Are you here?"

Mrs. Chan wasn't the first person in that village to peer in our windows. A lot of the Chinese villagers were so curious to find out how an American family lived that many times I looked up to see an audience staring in the window. They were especially fascinated when I disciplined the boys. Shutting the windows or curtains was out of the question because of Hong Kong's heat and humidity. Later I came to understand that Hong Kong people didn't have much of a sense of privacy, even with each other.

In spite of the fact that Mrs. Chan was at first annoying, I now had a friend and wasn't so lonely anymore. I also now had a place in the village—I was no longer the friendless stray.

Our relationship must have been even more trying for Mrs. Chan because of how basic my Cantonese was. Even though I had just finished studying the two-year Cantonese program at Chinese University, I was so verbally challenged that a two-year-old could have competed with me for who knew more words.

My first problem was to figure out what to say to my new friend. *How do you carry on a conversation with an adult woman when you have the vocabulary of a two-year-old?*

So I asked my tutor to teach me something to say to Mrs. Chan. Since one of my tutor's favorite subjects was how bad he thought the Hong Kong educational system was, he taught me a monologue of *his* thoughts about education that I memorized verbatim. What a stupid way to start a friendship!

One Saturday morning, Mrs. Chan and her boys, Ah-Fai and Ah-Gin, invited me, Nigel, and Adam out for dim sum. My sons, ages three and five, knew Cantonese better than I did at that point, and the four boys sat together laughing and teasing each other. By the time we had

---

[7] Mrs. Jeung was the Cantonese name I went by.

savored jellyfish marinated in sesame oil, spicy curried chicken's feet, and barbeque pork tucked in flaky pastries, I had already used up all my Cantonese vocabulary. There was a pause in the goofing, so I decided it was time to give my new friend some meaty opinions in the hope that we could start a discussion.

I cleared my throat. "The Hong Kong educational system stuffs knowledge down children's throats like force-feeding a goose for slaughter," I intoned in Cantonese. "It doesn't teach students to think, and it's not interactive. The students merely memorize what the teachers tell them and regurgitate it." Then I sat back, pleased with myself, hoping Mrs. Chan would now give her views on the education system. I didn't notice that all *I* had done was memorize and regurgitate the views of *my* teacher!

Mrs. Chan wrinkled up her nose, scrunched her eyebrows together and stared at me, trying to figure out what on earth I was talking about. It was a facial expression I was to become very familiar with during our years of friendship.

It turns out Mrs. Chan was illiterate! I only found this out a year later by accident, but that day, after eating dim sum, I didn't know she was uneducated and had spent little to no time in a classroom. She had no opinions on education, except that she was glad her kids could go to school.

§§§

Although illiterate, between the two of us, *she* was the one who was knowledgeable about what mattered in Hong Kong and *I* was the ignorant one. And she gave so much more to me than I gave to her, that is, until I led her to the Lord.

So much of what my sons and I learned about Chinese culture came from Mrs. Chan. At Chinese New Year she gave Nigel and Adam two red envelopes each. When they opened them, they found money inside! Ten Hong Kong dollars in each envelope! This was a beautiful Chinese tradition I knew nothing about. I quick went out, bought red envelopes, stuffed them with money, and gave them to her sons. After that, it was a tradition I followed with all the children we knew during Chinese New Year for as long as we lived in Hong Kong.

Mrs. Chan taught Nigel and Adam that during Chinese New Year they were supposed to greet everyone they knew by saying, "*Gong hei faat choih!*" ("Congratulations! Make a lot of money!"). She said we were congratulating the person for having lived through another year. But she told the boys, "Don't ever say, '*Laih sih dauh loih!*'" ('A red envelope is coming!')

"Why?" Nigel and Adam wanted to know.

"Just don't! It's naughty. People have to give you red envelopes with money in them if you say that."

Nigel's eyes lit up. What a great way to make money! So, for the two weeks of that Chinese New Year, Nigel stood outside from morning till night greeting in Cantonese every adult that passed by, "Congratulations, make a lot of money! A red envelope is coming!" Everyone had to give him red envelopes. He was so happy he made so much money that year.

Mrs. Chan wasn't very happy.

§§§

Later that spring Mrs. Chan arranged a tour to Mainland China for her Chinese friends and she invited me. She knew that I would feel a little out of place with her friends in China, so during the whole trip she always seated me next to her and took care of me.

It was a strange tour because so much of what we visited was pretentious.

We were taken to a song and dance performance at a kindergarten to show how amazing communist kindergartens are and how precocious children growing up in a communist country are. It was a beautiful performance, but the kids were obviously professionally trained, and they weren't even kindergarteners—they were all eight to ten years old! When I asked our tour guide about it, she wouldn't answer me. So the propaganda about Marxism fell flat. It was my first time seeing a Potemkin village.

Then we went to the Shenzhen Window of the World. This park had huge replicas of famous sites from around the world—from the Grand Canyon, Mt. Rushmore, and monuments in D.C., to the Pyramids, Taj Mahal, Angkor Wat, to Buckingham Palace and the

Eiffel Tower. So convenient to be able to see so many of the major tourist sites in the world in one park in China—a whole world tour! But I couldn't quite figure out why we would want to see these sites away from their original settings until it dawned on me—Marxist countries don't let their people freely travel to other countries (especially back then) because the people might escape. This was the best international travel some of these communist citizens would be able to enjoy!

One evening, close to the end of the tour, we were sitting at a banquet in a plush hotel in Guangzhou. Conversation was lively, but I wasn't enjoying it much. Although my Cantonese had kept improving from knowing Mrs. Chan, I still couldn't follow the fast-moving discussion of a group, so I remained mostly silent. Even more, I was embarrassed as her friends were having a great time, laughing and laughing, making me the brunt of their jokes since I couldn't understand what they were saying. Because Mrs. Chan was such a gentle person, she didn't put a stop to it.

I was so tired of being humiliated, and I wanted to get a break from being teased, so partway through the dinner I excused myself and went to the bathroom. After 20 minutes of enjoying solitude on the can, I heard Mrs. Chan rush into the washroom and cry out in panic, "Mrs. Jeung, Mrs. Jeung, are you here? Are you here?"

After I answered, I heard a sigh of relief.

When I opened the stall door, she looked me up and down several times to see if I was OK. Then she breathlessly she told me, "You were in the bathroom so long I was afraid you had been *sheng tang*! They do that in Mainland China."

Sheng tang literally means "slaughtered alive." Most of the victim's organs are removed for transplant while the person is still alive, and then the organs are sold.

At the time I thought my friend just had a fearful, lively imagination. Only years later, after we moved to Mainland China, did my Chinese friends there tell me that they actually knew people who had been *sheng tang*.

§§§

Back in Tin Sam Village, our four sons, despite the eight-year age gap, had become such good friends that the alley between our apartments often filled with laughter as they goofed around and played together. Whenever our family returned from vacation, Mrs. Chan would tell me, "It's so lonely when you're not here. It's awfully quiet."

Even after my Cantonese skills had improved enough to be able to talk with Mrs. Chan about the Lord, I didn't. Frankly, I didn't know how because she seemed to view life totally from the perspective of materialism, as if nothing but the material world existed. I couldn't find any connection points between her worldview and the Lord. So for the time being I just enjoyed letting our relationship grow.

Our friendship ended up deepening through gourmet cooking. Every evening I heard the loud sizzling of spattering grease from Mrs. Chan's wok as she stir-fried Cantonese gourmet delicacies for her family. One day, when a Chinese man from our church came to visit us, he pointed up at her kitchen window and commented, "Now there's an excellent cook. You can tell by all the grease covering the outside of the building under the kitchen window." I looked up at the black grease on the white tiles of the building, flowing the width of her window to a yard and a half down.

With its delicate, fresh flavors, and light sweetness, Hong Kong food was fast becoming my favorite, but I didn't know how to cook it. Since Mrs. Chan was always looking for ways to bless me, I asked her to teach me. After that, every day we went to the market, and she came over three times a week to teach me how to cook Cantonese-style—eel, squid, steamed fish with ginger and green onions, fungus, tofu with shitake mushrooms. The aromas of ginger, garlic, anise, and fresh sesame oil carefully added by an expert cook, were intoxicating.

§§§

But during all this friendship time, I couldn't stop thinking about how to talk with her about the Lord. Finally, the only thing I could come up with was to tell her about answers to prayer and what I was learning from my walk with the Lord. When she had a need, I said I'd pray for her. Although later with other Chinese friends this became an effective way to start conversations about God, it was totally ineffective with Mrs. Chan. What I was saying didn't make any sense to her because she had never heard about God or the spiritual world. She just kept wrinkling up her nose and scrunching up her eyebrows.

Sharing Christ with an illiterate woman who had never been exposed to a variety of ideas wasn't easy. It was going to take even more time, a closer relationship, and the Spirit opening her spiritual eyes before she could understand (I Corinthians 2:11-14).

§§§

I was growing more and more fond of Mrs. Chan, but sometimes our conversations would get stuck because she couldn't think outside her simple, Sinocentric perspective.

One day while we were cooking, I told her how much I love vegetables. She looked disgusted, "Oh, vegetables. They're just filler to make the meat taste good. Every part of an animal we eat benefits that same part of our body. For example, we need to eat the eyes, ears, noses, colons, and other internal organs of animals so those parts of our bodies will be healthy. But vegetables," she sneered, "they don't correspond to any part of our body, so we don't need them! They just taste good."

From eating the delicious food I was learning to cook, I had gained a little weight. So when we visited the States for a year, I tried very hard to lose. When we returned to Hong Kong, I triumphantly told Mrs. Chan, "I lost weight in the States!" She snorted. "Of course you would. They don't have Chinese food there."

Because she was uneducated, Mrs. Chan's perspectives were unadulterated by exposure to Western thinking, so through my friendship with her, my cultural perspectives naturally made a shift to traditional Chinese ways of thinking. It turned out that her being illiterate actually helped my acculturation to Chinese culture. The Lord had planned it, even for my sake.

§§§

Since April 15, 1989, everybody in Hong Kong had been closely watching the students protesting for freedom and democracy on Tiananmen Square in Beijing. All the Chinese I knew were rooting for the students, but we didn't know if they would be successful. It was hard for any of us to imagine how far this would spiral down.

When Mrs. Chan and I heard how the People's Liberation Army stationed in Beijing refused to obey orders from the Chinese government to deploy to Tiananmen Square, we cheered. But then the government brought in the PLA from other provinces, who had less attachment to Beijingers.

Early on June 4 Mrs. Chan pounded furiously on my door. "Turn on the TV! Turn on the TV!" she shouted as I unlocked the door. We watched in horror as tanks rolled into Tiananmen Square, then as the Goddess of Democracy (the students' replica of Lady Liberty) was torn down. We cried out when we heard the gunfire. Then we saw the panic-stricken students hauling their bleeding, injured friends on makeshift gurneys trying to get them to safety. Neither of us could stop weeping. It was inconceivable that the Chinese army would slaughter their own people like this. And although I had read the history of communist China, I had been naive to think they were incapable of doing this.

"How can we let this happen to our Chinese people and not do anything?" I asked through my tears.

"There's a protest march planned for this afternoon in Victoria Park. Would you like to go?"

Mrs. Chan's sons joined us as we boarded the packed MTR (subway) to join a million or more Hong Kongers as we all made our way to Victoria Park.

At the Causeway Bay MTR Station, where we disembarked, young men were selling white protest T-shirts lettered in red: 自由民主建中華 (Freedom and democracy will establish the Chinese people). We each bought one and wore them for the march.

Victoria Park was a sea of black hair. We shouted, cried, and protested in solidarity with the Chinese people in Tiananmen Square who were being slaughtered for aspiring to freedom.

Through my friendship with Mrs. Chan, the Chinese people were becoming my people.

§§§

I tried again to talk with Mrs. Chan about the Lord, but the more I did, the more it hit me that she had no religion whatsoever. She wasn't even an idol worshipper, which was the practice of most Hong Kong people. That's why she had no starting point for understanding about God or anything beyond the material world. On the subjects of God, prayer, worship, or the spiritual world, there was just a big gaping blank in her thinking. I kept trying to explain what I meant when I used the words *God* or *pray*, but I couldn't get through. She found the idea of a creator, especially one she couldn't see, completely baffling. How was I going to be able to communicate anything about God to her? The more I grew to love her, the more I ached for her to come to know the Lord.

Although I had started the ball rolling with Mrs. Chan, the Lord also had to use other people to get through to her.

Without my knowledge, Nigel began sharing about Jesus with Mrs. Chan's two sons. Nigel had committed his life to Christ when he was three, after he and I had a discussion about the millennium. It turns out, Nigel really wanted these two Chinese friends to come to know Jesus, too. I don't know what he said to them, but he finally invited them to the Cantonese church our family was planting, and they started attending regularly. It didn't take long before both of them decided to commit their lives to Jesus.

But very soon after that we noticed something strange about their faith. *Before* they "decided to follow Jesus" they had been attending church regularly, but *after* they "decided to follow Jesus" they only came to church sporadically, and when we asked them about it, their answer reminded us of how idol worshippers think. "Whenever we have a need, we go to church so God will help us. Why would we go to church except when we need something from God?"

Even though they weren't from an idol-worshipping family, they had absorbed the Hong Kong idol-worshipping attitude—offer your gift to the idol so you can get something from the idol. Otherwise, why bother worshipping the idol? Quid pro quo. What they offered the Christian God was church attendance; otherwise, he was peripheral to their lives—they only wanted a utilitarian relationship with him. It was pretty sub-Christian.

As we talked with them about their relationship with the Lord, they came to understand that he needed to be the center of their lives. Relationship with God is so much more than just getting what you want.

After Mrs. Chan's sons fully embraced Christ, *they* started telling her about Jesus, and they were able to get through where I couldn't. As a result, she finally began to show more interest in what I was saying about her creator God, and she started plying me with the questions that were confusing her.

Since we had eaten together many times, she had seen our family thank God for the food. It puzzled her. "It's so strange that you give *God* thanks for the food. Why would you thank him? What does he have to do with it? The farmer grew the crops; the hawker in the market sells the food to us. We should thank them. Thanking God makes no sense!" I told her that God made the seed and enables it to sprout, and that he sends the rain, and makes the sun shine on the crops. These were new ideas to her, but I could see she was starting to understand the concept of a creator and the spiritual world.

Then she said, "My husband was attacked by muggers a number of years ago. As a result of the attack, he has some brain damage and can't find a good job. How could God have let that happen?"

I told her that it wasn't God who attacked her husband, it was people. Then we talked about how sin came into the world and that's why people hurt each other. If God stopped us every time we were about to harm each other, he would be controlling us all the time, like a puppet-master. We also discussed what we can learn from suffering.

After we worked through her questions, I thought she was ready to become a Christian. Full of excitement I asked her, "Do you want to believe in Jesus now?"

"No! I will never, ever believe in Jesus!"

I was shocked and disappointed. I didn't ask her why she adamantly refused because I had already learned from her that Hong Kongers don't like people probing too deeply into their feelings. I just had to let it go.

After that, whenever I brought up the Lord she changed the subject, so I stopped saying anything about God, and I pretty much gave up hope that she would ever become a Christian. We continued to be close friends; we just didn't discuss what is most important in my life.

Four months later the Holy Spirit moved me to pray for her more fervently. Shortly after that, our church plant, which met in the public school of a low-income housing project, organized a "Health Day," where Christian doctors would answer attendees' medical questions one-on-one for free. Since we were emphasizing the health of the whole person, we held an evangelistic meeting that evening.

On Health Day I was so frustrated and discouraged I was moping around our apartment. Adam, who was four and a new believer, asked me why I was so blue. "This past week I invited a number of women from my English class to attend the evangelistic meeting, but one by one they turned me down. I really want them to come to know Jesus, but I don't seem to be able to make it happen."

"Mom, you have to think of David and Goliath. How could a boy kill a giant? Only because God helped him. It's the same with you and your friends who don't know the Lord. You can't make them become Christians, but God will help you!" As a young child, he had the faith I was struggling for. And it was almost like he was predicting what was about to happen.

Early that evening, as I walked out the door to go to the evangelistic meeting, Mrs. Chan's sons saw me through their kitchen window and asked where I was going. When I told them, their heads ducked back inside.

After walking the mile to church, I sat near the front of the auditorium. Toward the end of the service, I glanced behind me, and there was Mrs. Chan sitting by herself in the last row! I was shocked! Why was she here? I hadn't thought it was worth asking her to come.

After the meeting I walked back and sat next to her. "Mrs. Chan, how did you know about this meeting?"

"My sons told me. They made a deal with me that they would do the dishes if I would attend."

"But why did you even show up? You don't want to become a Christian." What a thing to say to somebody who just came to your church's evangelistic meeting!

She looked at me with determination. "I wouldn't have come if I didn't want to believe in Jesus."

I couldn't believe my ears! I thought back to all the fun times we had had together that led to this moment. Now I could see. What I hadn't realized earlier when Mrs. Chan refused to follow Christ was that the Lord needed me out of the picture for a while so he could reveal himself to her without my interference. And what Mrs. Chan needed was time to think about God without any pressure from me so it would be her own decision.

Right there in that back row, she committed her life to her creator God, the God who had once been so incomprehensible to her.

SUPERSTITION, DEMONS, AND GODS

1986-1994 Hong Kong; 1998, 2010 Mainland China

Mrs. Yip, a more distant neighbor in our Chinese village, invited me to her home one day, but it felt strange because we didn't seem to have normal conversation; instead, she was excited as she showed off how all the doors and windows in their luxurious apartment were *not* lined up with each other. I looked at her confused because I didn't know why that would be a bragging point. She explained in Cantonese that according to feng shui[8] any good luck that entered their home would be trapped and couldn't easily escape out the back door!

I thought about our apartment. The doors and windows in our home were strangely not lined up either—apparently it had also been built according to feng shui principles. But it didn't seem to have snared any good luck for our family; all it seemed to have trapped was the hot, humid air. There was no through breeze.

Then Mrs. Yip proudly told me how many thousands of dollars

---

[8] Feng shui is Chinese geomancy—a feng shui master advises how to arrange things in the environment to increase good luck. Feng shui literally means wind/water.

they had spent hiring a feng shui expert, who told them exactly where to place each piece of furniture to increase their good luck. She looked at me expectantly—I was supposed to praise the arrangement of the furniture and be awed by their wealth. But I didn't know what to say. It didn't look homey or comfortable; it just looked like a chaotic arrangement of furniture that was designed to obstruct people. Again, there were no thoroughfares people could walk along because the good luck might use them to escape. And, as far as their wealth, the Yip family had already given much of their money away—to the feng shui expert.

After that, Mrs. Yip walked me over to a huge rectangular goldfish tank—the largest tank I had ever seen in a home—which, in keeping with the expert advice of the feng shui master, had been placed awkwardly in the room, almost blocking a natural walkway, again to trap good luck.

She told me, "The word for fish, *yu*, is a homonym for plenty, *yu*. So the *fish* will bring us *plenty* of blessing!" That was when I first realized that Hong Kong people use puns to confer blessings or curses. I looked at the fish tank; I would have preferred an uncluttered walkway.

Then I put my foot in my mouth and asked a question I was curious about that nipped in the bud any possible blossoming friendship. "The train passes quite close to here, and many of the trains transport smelly pigs to market. When it passes, do you smell the pigs from your apartment?" Silence. I was quickly ushered out the door and never invited back again.

§§§

One of the things I did in order to adjust to Chinese culture and learn to behave in Chinese ways was to imitate my Chinese friends' actions. Like, when I visited a friend, I always brought a gift because my friends always brought me gifts when they visited. Or, when saying goodbye to friends who had come to visit, I learned to accompany them out the door, often walking a distance with them, to show how much I loved them, just like they did with me. Sometimes my imitation of them was as simple as laying my chopsticks across my bowl when I was finished eating, which was where they put their chopsticks to signify that they had eaten enough. I watched everything they did and said what they said to copy them, just like a child does.

I not only imitated them, I followed their instructions without understanding what I was doing. That wasn't always the best idea because some of my non-Christian friends' activities were religious, not just cultural, but I didn't always know the difference.

My husband and I struggled to know what was OK to participate in, and we often discussed the issues, trying to sort them out. We also relied on the views of the Chinese Christians in our church plant. The Christians in Hong Kong didn't compromise with the local religion; in fact, when an idol-worshipper decided to follow Jesus, at their baptism the church would hold an idol-burning ceremony to make clear that there would be no syncretism. So we found their views solid.

But at times I had to make a decision on the spur of the moment without their input.

One evening I returned from a funeral with my next-door neighbor. Just outside the gates of our apartment stairwells, she arranged some sticks and lit them on fire. Then she jumped over them. "Jump! Jump over them!" she ordered me. I jumped over the burning sticks. Only after I jumped did she tell me, "That's to make sure the demons from the funeral won't follow us into our homes!" I gasped. *Lord, what have I done? Please protect us!*

Then one Chinese New Year our neighbors set up tables outside with idols on them where they were burning incense and offering fruit as sacrifices. As our family passed by and greeted them, one of our neighbors offered me some fruit. "Here's some pomelo. Eat it!" I hesitated. My mind was racing. What was the significance of it? As far as I could tell, the pomelo had been offered to an idol. Paul said we could eat food offered to idols, as long as we're not participating in the idol worship and it's not a stumbling block to anyone.[9] But what meaning did my neighbor attribute to eating this fruit? Did she think I was participating in idol worship if I ate it? Or was she just being nice

---

[9] I Corinthians 8:4-13; 10:18-33.

and offering me a section of pomelo? I didn't know. But if it was merely a nice gesture, it would be rude to refuse. She kept pressuring me. Because I didn't think it was wrong, and because according to Hong Kong culture I couldn't be so blunt as to ask what the meaning of it was, I took some of the juicy, sweet pomelo and ate it. I also gave some to my husband who was with me, and he ate it, too. All I could think of was Eve offering the fruit to Adam. Was it spiritually dangerous to eat it?

I also participated in the cultural holidays, many of which were just innocent, fun celebrations, often based on a mythical story. I didn't participate in the obviously religious aspects of celebrations, but sometimes I had no idea there was any spiritual significance to some of the activities. For example, it was only after shooting off many firecrackers year after year during Chinese New Year that I found out that the *original* purpose of shooting off firecrackers was to scare away demons who might plague the New Year. Although that was where the tradition first came from, and some Hong Kongers still did it with that purpose in mind, others were merely having fun, with no religious overtones.

It was a difficult but very important dance—to be part of the culture so I could fit in as much as possible in order to be an influence for the Lord, but to not become spiritually polluted by the culture.

§§§

My non-Christian friends often honored me with gifts that were very meaningful to them. If the gift was religious and contrary to Christian beliefs, it was hard not to offend my friend, who was intending to show me love and respect.

One day Mrs. Jeh, one of my English students who hadn't yet come to believe in the Lord, was visiting our church for our going away party. She gave me what she considered a very special farewell gift—a pendant with an image of the Buddha carved into it! How did she not see a contradiction between Buddhism and Christianity? I had often talked with her about the Lord. Even though it was important to accept and value the gift from a friend, I destroyed it in the church office shortly after she gave it to me. Unfortunately, she walked into the office right after I had finished hammering it and was taken aback that I had destroyed her gift.

Another Chinese friend, Mrs. Lei, gave me an expensive set of 12 jade Chinese zodiac animal figures. Some American missionaries pressured me to throw them out, but those Americans weren't so fluent in Chinese. Since they probably didn't have such close friendships with the locals, did they really know the meaning of the Chinese zodiac? From talking with my local friends, I came to the conclusion that the Chinese zodiac didn't have the religious overtones that the Western zodiac has. So after praying about it, I kept the animal figures. And even that, did I get it right? It was important not to make a mistake about these things because demons can accompany religious objects and idols. (I Corinthians 10:19-21 hints at this.)

Then a close Chinese friend I had led to the Lord gave me a jade moth pendant on a silver necklace so I would have safe travels when I visited the States. I didn't wear it because I was afraid it was superstitious, but I offended her by not wearing it. I regret not wearing it because I think she was just trying to bless me in her cultural way.

§§§

But there were times when it wasn't we who were confused, it was the Chinese who were confused about *our* beliefs, as they viewed them from *their* religious perspective. One Christmas I was excited to display the beautiful large ceramic crèche I had brought from America because I was planning to use it to clearly explain to Mrs. Yu about Jesus. A few days after I displayed it on a bookshelf, Mrs. Yu came over. She was so happy to see the crèche. "Now I know who your idols are! I had been wondering what idols you worshipped!" I tried to explain to her that they were not idols and we didn't worship them, but she didn't believe me. The crèche had actually muddied my ability to tell her about Jesus. After she left, I put the crèche away and never displayed it again.

§§§

Much of Hong Kong culture was governed by blessings and curses.

Every time you spoke certain numbers in Cantonese, you were blessing or cursing the listener. Change the tone of the number four, *sei*, and you have the word for die, *sei.* If you said that number during Chinese New Year, you were almost putting a hex on the listener so they would die! Even though *we* didn't believe we were cursing them, it was very important to follow this custom so *they* wouldn't think we were cursing them. But the number eight, *baat*, was a blessing number because it rhymed with *faat*, which meant to grow or develop. *Faat daaht* means to make money, so when you said the number eight, you were blessing the listener that they would make a lot of money.

There were also some nefarious aspects of Hong Kong superstition that we had no control over that may have harmed us. We just had to depend on the Lord's protection. Outside our ground floor apartment on the window of the opposite apartment I noticed a mirror facing *our* home. I couldn't figure out why the mirror faced out toward the alley instead of being inside our neighbor's apartment so the family could use it. I asked a Chinese friend, and she said, "Any bad luck that is about to enter *their* home will instead be reflected by the mirror onto *your* apartment!" Our neighbors were effectively putting a curse on us! *Lord, please make any curses put on our family ineffective!*

§§§

To help us celebrate our first Chinese New Year in Hong Kong, a Chinese Christian friend wrote out blessings on strips of red paper. Special for our front door were four blessings—the panels for the lintel and the sides of the door were inscribed with very meaningful Christian blessings. A large diamond-shaped *fuk* (福 the blessing character) was to be fastened to the center of the door. My friend instructed me to place the *fuk* upside down, like an upside down bowl of blessing pouring out its contents.

Since I couldn't read Chinese yet, I fastened the rest of the blessings, one on each door inside our apartment, without knowing what they said. After I had pasted all the blessings, my friend visited. When she passed the blessing on the bathroom door, she started laughing. "You know what blessing you put on the bathroom door?" She snickered. "It says, 'May we have abundance!'" She looked at the toilet and burst out laughing again.

THE BUDDHIST MATRIARCH AND HER FAMILY

1991-1994, Hong Kong

"*Sihk jo faahn meih a*?" ("Have you eaten yet?") This familiar Cantonese greeting, which came from a history of national starvation, jarred me out of my thoughts as I headed for the market pulling my red cart. A short, old, wrinkled woman smiled as she strained to look up at me. Her L-shaped hunched back had stolen what little height she originally had—bent over, she was only three feet tall!

Everyone called her *Bou Louh Taai* (Old Mrs. Boe), and she was the 85-year-old Buddhist[10] matriarch of one of the extended families in our village. I was 50 years her younger. *Jeung Taai* (Mrs. Jeung) was what everyone in the village called me.

"I've eaten. And you?" I replied.

"I've eaten." She shuffled along trying to keep pace with me. Old Mrs. Boe had decided to become friends with me.

The age, cultural, and religious barriers between us were great, but

---

[10] This family's Buddhism was a mix of Hong Kong Buddhism—idol and ancestor worship—and orthodox Buddhism.

we quickly grew to love each other. After that first walk, every other morning I heard her weathered voice cry out urgently in Cantonese as she craned her neck sideways to look up at the porch of our third-floor apartment. "Mrs. Jeung, Mrs. Jeung, come! *Come quick!*" Whenever I heard her call, I ran down the stairs and we headed out for a walk.

She always hurried me out of the village as fast as she could walk, and I finally figured out why. She was trying to hide our friendship from her Buddhist family, and that was the reason for the urgency—she was afraid her family would object to her friendship with a Christian. She often led me to the neighboring housing estate where we talked in the shade, sitting on the cement wall that encircled the one tree, surrounded by tightly packed 35-story skyscrapers.

As the matriarch, Mrs. Boe was officially in charge of the idol and ancestor worship for her extended family, and I had seen her offering sacrifices to the departed spirits during the Ghost Festival. But I don't think she had ever heard about her creator God before, and as I started to tell her about him, she received what I had to say like a cool spring of water on a sweltering hot day. Her interest made it obvious that she was not the engine behind her family's Buddhist worship. The enforcer was her daughter, Mrs. Lam.

§§§

Before Old Mrs. Boe and I became friends, Nigel (eight) and Adam (six) had already become friends with her grandson, seven-year-old Ah-Hoe, Mrs. Lam's son.

The boys spoke Cantonese with each other as they palled around the village, and played on the hillside behind the village. Nigel and Adam took Ah-Hoe to their secret *gei deih* (military base), which they had made out of our moving crate and set up in a large empty field of tall grass. They inducted him into the *Gwok Jai Yauh Gik Deui* (International Guerrilla Forces), a very secret organization that provided military training for its inductees. Nigel was the General. This was a distinctly American way of playing; Hong Kong kids didn't play games like this until our kids taught them.

When the Mid-Autumn Festival arrived, late in the evening you would find the three of them on the hillside occupied with a dangerous

Mid-Autumn Festival activity that many of the Hong Kong children were involved in—*bou laahp* (boiling wax). After our family lit the candles in the Mid-Autumn Festival lanterns, ate mooncakes, and went to our flat roof to gaze at the full moon, one of our kids would tuck the empty mooncake tin and dozens of candles under his jacket, and the two of them would sneak outside. Up on the hillside, Ah-Hoe joined them. They lit the candles in the tin and let them burn down until the tin was full of flaming hot molten wax. Then one of the kids would throw water onto the wax, which would explode into a boiling cloud of wax rising several meters in the air. The kids had to stand way back so they wouldn't get burned. They found the danger thrilling.

One day in December, when Ah-Hoe came over to play with the boys, I was in our bedroom stamping leather to make a wallet for Justin's Christmas gift. I didn't want anyone to see the gift or what I was doing, so when Ah-Hoe passed by the bedroom and greeted me, I shouted, "Don't come in! Don't come in!"

He thought I was angry. "Oh, you must be reading the Bible, that's why you're so angry. My mother gets like that when she's reading the Buddhist scriptures."

"No, I'm not reading the Bible," I objected. "I'm making a secret Christmas gift and I don't want anyone to find out. That's why you can't come in." I didn't want him to think that reading the Bible made me an angry person. But apparently reading the Buddhist scriptures made his mother irritable.

Then one day I noticed that Nigel and Adam were exceptionally happy and were playing with brand-new toys that we hadn't bought them. I asked them where the toys came from. Nigel couldn't stop grinning. "Ah-Hoe took us to the store and told us he would buy us any toys we wanted. Aren't these great toys! He took us to the store yesterday, too. I'll show you what he bought us yesterday."

Red flags were going up in my mind. "Where did Ah-Hoe get so much money?"

"He took it from his father's drawer. He said it's OK. Look at how this army guy can actually shoot his gun."

"Boys, I think you need to put these toys away until we find out where this money came from."

"Do we have to?"

I spent the next day debating what to do, and I talked with Justin about it. If it were my kid that had taken my money, I would want to be told. I was a little scared because I had never spoken with Ah-Hoe's father, Mr. Lam, and he seemed a little stern.

Just before supper that evening, I bumped into Mr. Lam at the entrance to the village and told him about the toys Ah-Hoe had given my sons and where he said the money came from. Mr. Lam showed no emotion; he just thanked me.

What happened next I didn't expect.

The following evening Mrs. Lam rang our doorbell. "Could you, Nigel, and Adam come over to our home?" she asked in Cantonese. I was surprised because we had never been invited to their home before.

When we entered their apartment, Ah-Hoe was standing in the corner, grimacing, shifting from one foot to the other and back again. After the Lams asked us to sit, I looked at Ah-Hoe, expecting him to sit, too. "I can't sit. It hurts too bad. My father beat me!"

I was horrified—although I had never expected a severe beating to be the outcome of my telling Mr. Lam about his son's theft, I now felt like I was complicit in the beating.

As we talked about the problem, I tried to downplay Ah-Hoe's indiscretion. In his childish way, he had tried to be kind to my sons. But nobody seemed to care about Ah-Hoe's kindness.

I was also trying to figure out how to turn the conversation around to share about Christ.

Then Mrs. Lam spoke sternly to Ah-Hoe. "Now don't you go thinking that Christianity is better than Buddhism because of all this. We know that Mrs. Jeung, Nigel, and Adam are all Christians, but just because they're good, kind people that doesn't mean Christianity is better. We are Buddhists and Buddhism is better!"

I had no idea how to be a witness for Christ after that. But maybe we already had been—Ah-Hoe's mother had seen Christ in us! And I suspected that Nigel and Adam had been telling Ah-Hoe about the Lord.

§§§

All along, for the three years I had known her, I had been telling Old Mrs. Boe about God, and I thought it was time for her to hear a clear presentation of the gospel from a Hong Kong person to make sure she understood. A nearby Christian retirement home, where I often played guitar for the deaf residents, was going to hold an evangelistic meeting, so I invited her to accompany me. Surprisingly she agreed to go!

The afternoon the meeting was to be held, while I was fixing my hair, the doorbell rang. After patting a few curls, I raced down the three flights, and opened the door, but no one was there!

By the time I reached the top of the three flights, the doorbell rang again. I ran back down the stairs, opened the door, but again I couldn't see anyone anywhere near our building.

I was getting fed up. The doorbell rang two more times, with me running down the stairs each time, but on the fourth time when I opened the door, 88-year-old Mrs. Boe was standing there, nervously glancing to the left, to the right, to the left again. "Let's go right away!" she said. "I can't let my family see you taking me to a Christian meeting! Every time I rang your doorbell, someone passed by and I had to sneak away and hide. Let's go, quick!"

At the meeting, the speaker gave a very down-home presentation of the gospel. I turned to Mrs. Boe, "Did you understand?"

"No."

So after the meeting I asked the speaker to sit down with us and present the gospel one-on-one to my friend so she could understand it. After explaining how to become a Christian, he pulled a flashlight out of his pocket. "Our lives are like this flashlight." He moved the switch, but it didn't shine. Then he took a battery out of his pocket and put it in the flashlight. "God is like the battery. When he comes into our lives then we shine." He flipped the switch and the flashlight turned on.

I took Mrs. Boe home by taxi, and as we neared our village she became visibly afraid. "Stop!" she shouted. "Let me out here. I'll walk the rest of the way. I can't let anyone see me!"

I had planned to follow up with her to see whether she had decided to believe in Jesus, but before I got the chance, Mrs. Boe fell in the market and broke her hip. Her family didn't tell me, so I wasn't able to visit my friend in the hospital. I couldn't comfort her and ask if she wanted to follow Jesus. I've wondered if her family purposely didn't tell me so I couldn't lead her to Christ in the hospital. But since she had been so secretive with them, I doubt they realized how attracted she was to Jesus and that she already did know how to become a Christian.

Two weeks later Mrs. Boe died! She left a big hole in my life. I was so glad I had brought her to the evangelistic meeting before she passed away.

Had this old Buddhist matriarch aligned herself with Christ as she lay in pain in the hospital bed? Did the Lord finish the work he was doing in her life in drawing her to himself? I hope so. I would love to take more walks with her in heaven. I'm sure she will be a little taller and it will be easier for her to look me in the face. Also, she won't have to sneak anymore to be with me!

Her daughter-in-law, "Young Mrs. Boe," who was about 50 years old, told me about her mother-in-law's passing and invited me to the funeral. They held a Buddhist funeral with rented Buddhist monks loudly chanting and clanging cymbals. A grating cacophony of noise. The monks made sure everyone who attended worshipped Old Mrs. Boe. We were all supposed to go to the front, light incense, and kowtow to her while holding the incense. A kowtow is a deep bow from the waist.

Before the funeral I had asked some Chinese Christian friends from our church how I should conduct myself at the Buddhist funeral. "Don't light the incense and don't kowtow. As Christians we mustn't worship the dead!" When I asked what I should do instead, they said, "At the front, bow only your head and pray to the Lord." It was a way to respect the Buddhist customs while taking a stand for Jesus.

The Boes and Lams also respected my faith and didn't allow the monks to try to force me to worship my friend.

After I prayed to Jesus in front of the chanting Buddhist monks and the burning incense, Young Mrs. Boe grabbed my arm and, without a word, led me back to the little room behind the incense where Old Mrs. Boe's body was lying in the coffin. Only the family and I, her close friend, were allowed to go back there.

Standing a couple meters from the coffin, in an eerie voice, Young

Mrs. Boe spoke to Old Mrs. Boe's ghost, "Old Mrs. Boe, Old Mrs. Boe, Mrs. Jeung is here. Mrs. Jeung has come to see you."

Then she paused and stared at me. She was waiting for me to speak to Old Mrs. Boe's ghost! I didn't know what to do.

I didn't say a word.

The Chinese Christians had told me how to conduct myself during a Buddhist funeral, but they never told me what I should do if I was expected to talk with my friend's ghost.

A CHILD'S COSTLY FAITH

1992, Hong Kong

Nigel and Adam, now nine and seven, were having fun playing on the wine-colored couch in our living room while we listened to an album by Michael Card.

Suddenly Adam jumped up and ran down the hall to Justin's and my bedroom. As he ran he looked over his shoulder, tears streaming down his face. "Mom, I need to talk to you!"

As we sat together on the bed, Adam poured out his heart to me. "There's a Chinese girl in my class, her name is Lisa. She's not real smart. Do you know what I mean, Mom?"

"You mean she was born that way?"

"Yeah, that's right. I played with her because she has no friends."

I looked at my boy with new eyes. He had only been a believer for four years, but I saw the signs—he had the gift of mercy. That gift can be quite a burden because it may give you the courage and determination to help people in need regardless of the cost to yourself. I didn't say anything to him; I let him continue his story, which I suspected was momentous.

His breath caught like he was trying not to cry anymore. "Well, you know, it's kind of boring playing with her. But it was OK until a month ago. I don't know what happened, but all the kids started making fun of her, and they won't stop. Then they started making fun of me because I was playing with her. They said I was stupid." His tears started again. I wrapped my arms around him and gently rocked him until he could continue.

"So I started making fun of her, too." He sobbed. "I know it's wrong and that it hurts Jesus. The song we were listening to made me realize it. But I don't know what to do! If I don't make fun of her, they'll make fun of me."

We prayed together that he would have the courage to be kind to Lisa.

After some thought, he straightened his shoulders and looked determined. "I'm not going to make fun of her. I have to do that for Jesus!" Then he raced back to the living room to play again.

A week later I asked him about it. His eyes clouded over and his lips quivered. "I'm still making fun of her."

It was the last month of second grade. I made sure I didn't ask him often, even though I was praying fervently, but every time he gave me the same answer. I knew that he, too, was praying that he would have courage.

After summer break, a month into third grade, Adam came to me while I was cooking one evening. I turned off the fire, knelt down to his height, and put my hands on his shoulders.

He looked sad. "Mom, I'm not making fun of Lisa anymore. The whole school has turned against me. Everyone makes fun of me all the time now. Being her friend is the right thing to do, but it hurts. The reason why it was so hard for me to stop making fun of her before is that I knew this would happen. I knew everyone would make fun of me." He sighed.

My heart ached hearing this.

The boys were attending a British-run primary school with British curriculum and teachers, but the students, almost without exception, were Chinese. We had enrolled them in this school so they could be educated in English, but still keep their fluency in Cantonese. Adam spoke Cantonese with his classmates because he said that was easier than English, but he was the only white kid in his class, which made him the outlier, so it was even more fun to pick on him.

At the time I didn't realize the extent of his pain or how long it would take this scar to heal. But what I also didn't know was how much internal strength it would develop in him. He told me only recently that living through those two years taught him that he could survive anything. He has an ability now to stand up against any evil that confronts him.

But during that time, he didn't talk to me again about how the kids were treating him. Every afternoon, when the boys arrived home from school, we'd sit together on the flat roof of our apartment eating fresh baked cookies and I'd ask them about their day. Without displaying any emotion, Adam would always reply, "I don't remember. Sitting in the train and the bus coming home is my 'forgetting time.' After that I can't remember what they did to me at school."

One day, when I was visiting the school, a teacher's aide spotted me. "You're Adam's mother, aren't you? I work with Lisa, and Adam has been a lifesaver for her. She couldn't have coped if it weren't for Adam's friendship."

Then one day Adam came home quite upset. "I made a mistake on my homework. The teacher makes us line up and give it to her, but if there's anything wrong with our homework, she announces it to the whole class to shame us. Her shaming me in front of the class is making everything worse. Now the kids are making fun of me even more!"

"Dad and I will talk to your teacher, Adam."

A few days later Justin and I went in to see his teacher, Mrs. Hyde. We sat down in front of her desk and told her what Adam was doing for Lisa and how all the kids were mocking him for it. "He's doing this because he loves Jesus," I added. "Would it be possible for you to not publicly announce if something's wrong with his homework? It's making it even harder for him—the kids are making fun of him even more."

Mrs. Hyde was shaken by what we told her. With tears in her eyes, she said, "I, too, am a follower of Jesus, but I don't think it shows. Hearing what you've told me, I'm learning from Adam that I need to live out my faith and be willing to pay the price of following the Lord. I want to change. Thank you so much for telling me this.

"And, about the homework, if he makes a mistake, I'll talk to him privately."

CHAIN REACTION

1995-2014, Hong Kong

Jazelle looked up at me with a confused expression on her face and asked in Cantonese, "Why does God hate his children so much? I'm seriously thinking about becoming a Christian, but this is the one thing that's stopping me. Christians face so much suffering. It looks like God is treating them really bad."

Jazelle, Adam, and I were returning home on the MTR (subway) from the large evangelistic meeting I had invited her to. Only a month earlier, she had shown up out of the blue at our small church plant, which worshipped in the activity room of a community center. The room was very plain—the walls and floors were cement, painted white, and behind the podium hung a red velvet curtain signifying that area as the stage.

I noticed Jazelle immediately when she walked in, with her long silky hair, lively eyes, and high cheekbones. She was taller than most Hong Kong people, and she carried herself with grace.

At the end of the service, I rushed over to meet her. In her low, husky voice, she told me that she was actually from Guangdong Province in Mainland China. Her husband, Leon, was from Hong

Kong; they had met and married in Guangdong, then he brought her down to Hong Kong to live.

Over the next month, I visited Jazelle several times at her apartment and shared with her about the Lord, but she didn't show any interest. That wasn't unexpected because most people weren't interested in hearing about the Lord. But I decided to invite her to a citywide evangelistic meeting anyway, and I was surprised she agreed to go.

Now, on the MTR, I was overwhelmed at her saying she *did* want to believe in Jesus, and she had just told me what was preventing her. I thought back to when I had shared the gospel with her. If only I had asked more questions instead of just telling her what I thought she needed to know about Jesus, I might have found out what was preventing her from believing. Then I could have dealt with her real questions instead of guessing what she needed to hear and getting a stone-faced response.

But what especially amazed me was that I had just spent a whole year asking the Lord *almost the same exact question* she asked me, as a result of a terrible trial our family was going through! Had the Lord matched us up? Was I the person he wanted to use because of my own suffering and questioning?

What had happened to one of our sons was so horrific that for a few weeks I was afraid to feel anything—I didn't think I could go on if I faced what happened. So I took time off and listened to audio novels nonstop in order to block out reality. I vigilantly tried to make sure there was no gap between novels so a thought couldn't creep in.

The gash in my soul was so deep I couldn't pray in a normal way because then I would have needed to think and feel. So once every day I looked up to heaven and prayed the same brief prayer as fast as I could before any thoughts could go through my mind. "*Help!*" The Lord heard my truncated, traumatized prayer.

After a couple of weeks, I was able to dance a prayer, using my hands and body instead of words to tell the Lord what happened and how I felt. Usually, the dance ended with me sobbing on the floor.

But after I was finally able to face the situation, I needed to understand why God would let our family—his children—suffer so badly. When the Lord broke me (see "Broken" in *Dragon Ride*), he started me on the journey of understanding the purpose of suffering, as he stripped away my false beliefs one by one and replaced them with his thinking. But during that dark night of the soul, the time my son was suffering, I frequently meditated on I Peter and Hebrews 12, trying to make sense of Christian suffering.

So when Jazelle asked me this question on the subway, the thoughts I shared came out of the crucible of studying Scripture through the lens of emotional pain. I told her, "God disciplines us just like you as a mother discipline your son because you love him so much. God uses hardship to teach us, but it can be quite painful to go through." As I said this, I tried to hide the pain I could feel showing on my face. "But if we allow ourselves to be trained by God's discipline, we'll become righteous, and our hearts will find peace."[11]

"That makes sense," she said. "I've never understood the answer to that question, and I certainly didn't want to become God's child if he's mean to his children." We didn't say much for the rest of the ride because she was looking off into the distance, deep in thought.

The following day, Sunday, I sat next to Jazelle in our church plant. She was so excited she was jumpy. She whispered to me, "Now that you answered my question, I want to become a Christian! How do I do it? Am I supposed to run up to the front and tell everybody I've decided to follow Jesus? Is that how a person becomes a Christian? What do I do? Tell me!" She couldn't take one more minute without Jesus.

I probably should have taken her to a side room and introduced her to Jesus immediately, but instead I tried to calm her down enough so she could sit through the worship service. After the service, she committed her life to Christ.

Who would have guessed that the Lord could use my intense emotional pain to bring someone to faith? But it only happened because I had struggled with the Scriptures for answers.

After that, every week I went to Jazelle's apartment to disciple her. This was the first time she had read the Bible or heard much about the Christian faith, so everything was completely new to her, but she was

---

[11] See Hebrews 12:5-11.

so fired up about knowing Jesus that she read the whole Bible in a few months.

Jazelle's eight-year-old son, Tyson, often showed up while I was visiting. It seems he knew when I was supposed to come and he showed up on purpose to see me. We didn't say anything to each other; he would just stand for a while in the middle of the living room staring at me and smiling. He had the most beautiful smile I have ever seen and I had a very special love for Tyson. I had always thought he was a great, well-behaved kid, but what he intimated to me later made me wonder if he might have been involved in criminal activities, even at such a young age. That wasn't so uncommon in Hong Kong in areas where the Triads[12] were active.

Jazelle visited her family in Mainland China and told them all about Jesus and how she had come to believe in him. She was so passionate about sharing Christ with atheists in the Mainland that after she returned she told me, "Since I'm married, I don't have enough freedom to serve God. I'm going to divorce Leon so I can travel throughout China to share the gospel!"

I shuddered. "Jazelle, you can't divorce your husband in order to serve God! God hates divorce.[13] You can't serve God by disobeying him."

She decided to stay in her marriage, even though it would restrict her in sharing the gospel. In the meantime, she grew to love her husband, and she shared with him about Jesus.

A few months after Jazelle committed her life to Christ, our family moved from Hong Kong back to the States for a year. Jazelle was baptized a month after I left. It was two years before I saw her again. We had already moved to Mainland China and we were returning to Hong Kong for the July 1, 1997 turnover of Hong Kong from Britain to Mainland China.

I couldn't wait to see all my old Chinese friends, but as soon as I walked into the church, Jazelle ran up to me, grabbed my arm and pulled me over to her husband, Leon.

---

[12] Triads are Chinese organized crime groups.

[13] See Matthew 19:4-6; Malachi 2:16.

"Leon has something he wants to tell you, Grace," Jazelle turned toward Leon, her face beaming.

"Grace, I, too, have decided to follow Jesus! No one in the church knows. You are the only one I'm willing to tell. It's a secret!"

I was grinning from ear to ear. "Jazelle never told me."

She turned back to me. "He's been waiting for you to return to Hong Kong so he could tell you himself!"

I didn't see her again until 17 years later, in 2014, when we visited Hong Kong in order to change my visa for the Mainland. Our little church plant that had started in 1991 with 19 people and had only 60 when we left in 1995 had grown to 600 people! It was now meeting in a large public school auditorium. When Justin saw the size of the church, he laughed. "It took us leaving for the church to grow well!"

Many members from our original church plant core group came together to take us to the "best seafood restaurant in all of Hong Kong" to celebrate our visit. Shortly after Justin and I walked into the restaurant, Jazelle and Tyson, her son, who was now in his late 20s, came in and stood next to me. Jazelle looked older, and her long black hair was now cut in a pixie. Tyson still had the most beautiful smile I have ever seen. I was speechless seeing them again.

The 15 of us sat at a large round table to eat a 20-course dinner of lobster, crab, calamari, grouper, clams, oysters ... You can't beat Hong Kong for delicious seafood.

Tyson made sure he sat next to me. "Grace, I believe in Jesus now," he told me in Cantonese as he flashed his beautiful smile at me. "I have longed to see you so I could tell you. I am really glad you came back to Hong Kong for a visit because there's so much to tell you.

"I work as a counselor at a public school, and I have a lot of opportunities to share Christ with the students! They need to know the Lord, too.

"I'm looking for a woman to marry—someone who loves the Lord as much as I do. And I plan to teach my children about God and bring them to church so they will love Jesus, too."

Tears came to my eyes. Then I asked him, "When you were little, I especially loved you. Did you know?"

"Did I know?" He laughed. "Your love meant so much to me,

especially with what I was involved in when I was eight."

I wondered if my love had helped him come to faith in Jesus, even though we had had a wordless friendship.

Then Jazelle leaned forward so she could talk to me around Tyson. "My husband is with the Lord now. I have been able to share about Jesus with my whole extended family in China, and all of them have come to believe!"

The kingdom of heaven is like a chain reaction.[14]

[14] Matthew 13:33.

HONG KONG CHURCH LOVE

1991-1995, USA, Hong Kong

"They *never* should have taken those two beautiful little boys to Hong Kong. That's no place to raise children!" The condescending voice of disdain reached my ears in the stall of the women's bathroom of a retirement home in North Carolina.

"What *were* they thinking!" shrilled another woman.

I was at my father-in-law's funeral, and I had stopped in the bathroom only to overhear two old gossips haranguing about Justin's and my decision to serve as missionaries in Hong Kong. They showed no interest in using the bathroom except as a hideout for bad-mouthing us.

After I finished, I calmly opened the stall door, walked toward them and smiled. Their faces registered shock and embarrassment.

So America is the only good place to raise a child?

Certainly, there were difficulties and dangers in Hong Kong, but if I had thought the two women cared to listen, I would have told them *good* stories about the boys growing up in Hong Kong.

Like the many times Nigel and Adam, along with their Chinese friends, made gliders, which they intended to use to fly off the flat roof of our apartment. (I made sure that didn't happen.) In Hong Kong, in the second town where we lived, there was a lot of open, unclaimed space, so they hauled a small shipping crate into an empty field of tall grass to serve as a military base for playing with their Chinese friends. They furnished it with the amenities of a soldier and conducted military exercises there. They created a special language called Mouse Language—a monosyllabic language like Cantonese, which used the tones of Cantonese but was made up of only vowels. And they wrote so many stories—the boys had two languages to write stories in!

But what I would have emphasized to the women in North Carolina was how much our Cantonese church loved our kids.

When the boys were nine and seven, they told me they needed a raft. After finding a merchandise pallet and hauling it up the four floors to our flat roof, Nigel looked up at me sadly and said, "It won't float. How do we get it to float?" He looked back down at the pallet. "I know! It needs air underneath it. Empty soda bottles will do that."

The very next Sunday at our Chinese church plant, Nigel excitedly urged everyone in Cantonese, "Drink as much soda as you can and bring me the empty bottles! I need them for the raft Adam and I are building."

So the whole church went on a drinking spree, and everyone brought all their empty bottles to church and gave them to Nigel.

Then a couple of the church leaders came up to our roof to inspect the raft to see how it was coming along. They had never seen anything like it, and they couldn't stop laughing and goofing with Nigel and Adam. After that, small groups of people from our church kept showing up at our home to see the raft and joke with the boys about it. Nigel and Adam were so excited showing off their project to all these Chinese people they loved.

Finally, enough soda had been drunk, the bottles were all strapped to the bottom of the pallet, and on a chilly December afternoon a triangular sail made out of polypropylene fabric was raised up on a pole, and the raft was ready to sail.

We lived on a peninsula, over the hill from Ching Seui Wan (Clear Water Bay). We hauled the raft there, then I waded into the cold winter water, chest deep to make sure the boys would be safe while they sailed their raft. It not only floated, it sort-of sailed!

When we were about to move from Hong Kong, the church asked each of our boys what special thing they would like to do with the church for their goodbye. Anything!

Nigel loved basketball and wanted to teach the church how to shoot a basket. So, on the set day, in the room where we worshipped, everyone moved all the chairs to the side to form a basketball court. Someone set up a hoop, and basketball training was on.

Adam loved spicy hot foods, so he wanted to have a contest to see who could eat the spiciest foods. There actually is a Cantonese word for such a contest—*dao laaht*! So the church people ate at the spiciest restaurants they could find, and when they tasted a spicy hot dish they could barely tolerate, they asked the manager if they could have a little baggie of the spicy sauce. Armed with all these baggies, on the appointed day, the chairs in the "sanctuary" were again pushed to the side, and a table was set up—Adam on one side, the challengers on the other, with the baggies in the center. Every contestant had to eat a spoonful of each hot sauce straight up.

A number of burned mouths later, the Chinese people in our church had made their point: they loved our kids and would miss them dearly. And, with love like this, I would say Hong Kong was a fine place to raise our boys.

MAINLAND CHINA

1996-2015

We loved Hong Kong,
but Justin felt called to Mainland China,
so we moved to the Mainland—first to Wuran,
and later we lived in Re Dai, then Kao Shan.

To live in the Mainland, we needed student or work visas.
That meant that in addition to being employed
by the mission agency,
we were either full-time students or one of us had a job.

First, we studied Mandarin for three years,
and after that, Justin worked a variety of jobs.

We used Mandarin for most of our ministry in the Mainland.
Justin taught Bible school level courses to house church leaders.
We also led Bible studies for college students.
My main ministry was sharing the gospel,
which included leading evangelistic discussion groups
for atheist and Buddhist college students.

In the Mainland,
it was a joy getting to know the Chinese people and their culture,
but we faced a lot of difficulties
dealing with the police, Marxism, predators,
and our own inadequacies.

After our sons, Nigel and Adam, graduated from high school,
they returned to the States for college and work.
Their adjustment to the U.S. was hard.
But the Lord was with all of us!

MARKET PHOBIA

1996-1997, Wuran

For the whole week after we arrived in Mainland China, the only thing our family had to eat for every meal was peanut butter and jelly sandwiches. That was the only food I could find since I didn't know the language. I had discovered the peanut butter, jelly, and cardboard-like bread in a hole-in-the-wall store; the locals seemed to buy everything they needed from the market. I hadn't seen a grocery store.

There was no way around it—I was going to have to learn to buy food in the market even before language school started, so I asked our new Chinese friend, Peter,[15] to teach me a little market Mandarin. *Duo shao qian?* (How much does it cost?) *Yi, er, san, si, wu, liu, qi, ba, jiu, shi* (1, 2, 3, 4, 5, 6, 7, 8, 9, 10). Each word had its tone.

I was a little apprehensive because the first time I had entered a market in Hong Kong, I was so horrified to see birds being skinned alive that I backed up into a side of beef covered in flies that was hanging from a meat hook. I hoped the market experience in Mainland China would be better. But regardless, I had to find something more

---

[15] This is Peter from several stories in *Dragon Ride*.

than peanut butter and jelly to serve my family.

When I walked onto the market street in Wuran, what first caught my eye was garbage and rotting food strewn everywhere. This street had once been pretty—leafy green tree branches were leaning over it, meeting in the center. But hawkers had turned it into a filthy walking street with makeshift tables set up on both sides.

Each table held only a sparse amount of a single type of food, because the vendors were so poor they didn't have much to stock. A few vegetables. Fruit. Slabs of pork. Cuts of beef. A large box of eggs. Dried vegetables. Pickled vegetables. Bottles of soy and other sauces. On the ground were tubs of plump swimming fish, cages of skinny chickens, gunny sacks of white rice, burlap bags of beans. And behind each table, tub, cage, or sack stood a grimy, gruff man in filthy, coarse clothes.

The whole place looked uninviting; no one smiled or laughed. And the hawkers stared impassively at my white face—it seemed they had never seen a Westerner before, and they didn't care to meet one.

I braced myself and walked up to the first vegetable table. Oh no. I had never seen these vegetables before and I had no idea how to cook them.

Then I realized another problem—there weren't any prices on the vegetables. In fact, as I glanced around, I saw that none of the tables had prices on any of the items! This was going to be more difficult than I had expected.

Moving on to the next vegetable vendor, I saw a head of broccoli. I was so excited to see a vegetable I recognized. I pointed at the broccoli and asked, *"Duo shao qian?"* ("How much does it cost?") Had I said it right? Could he understand me?

The man sneered and didn't answer. Instead, he held out on a string what looked like a scale—a rod with a plate hanging from one end and a weight suspended from the other. The rod had markings cut into the metal all along it. He put the broccoli on the plate and moved the string fulcrum along the markings on the rod.

How was I supposed to know how much it weighed? And I didn't even know the cost per whatever weight measurement he was using. He could cheat me any way he wanted!

The vendor looked up at me and smiled a sleazy smile. He said two syllables, but the only syllable I understood was *si* (four). I froze. I had forgotten to learn the names of the denominations of money! That must have been the other syllable.

I pulled several bills from my purse. Chinese money is not only colorful, but the more value a bill has, the bigger it is. I decided to give him four of the green bills, the second smallest bill—four *kuai*, which was about 50 cents.

He smirked and quickly thrust my four *kuai* into his shirt pocket. From his reaction I realized that I had probably given him ten times what he had asked for; I should have given him four of the brown bills, the smallest bill. That would have been four *mao*, which was about five cents. (Most things in China were very cheap at that time. Our salary was also very low.)

Embarrassed, I took the broccoli and walked on. Tension was building inside me; I was sure word would spread in the market that I didn't know how to buy anything, and on my next trip the hawkers would overcharge me. But at least I had succeeded in buying some broccoli for my family to eat!

As I passed the pork and beef tables, the thick smell of raw meat filled my nostrils. I sighed. Buying meat was out of the question since I had no idea how to order it.

Looking at the other tables, it was hard to get up the courage to try again. That is, until I spotted a table of mangoes! Mangoes in Asia are nothing like mangoes in America. If you imagine what a mango might be like in heaven, well, that's what mangoes in Asia taste like—a little tart, a little sweet, and a rich, full mango flavor. I had to have some mangoes, so I walked over to the mango table.

"*Duo shao qian*?" ("How much does it cost?")

Like the broccoli vender, this man also sneered and didn't answer me. He began stacking a few orangey-golden mangoes onto his scale. I could smell the sweet mango from where I was standing.

"*Duo shao qian*?" I repeated.

He replied with three syllables, but I only understood *si* (four), which to my surprise he said twice! It was only later that I found out that in the Wuran dialect of Mandarin the number ten sounds identical to four. Who would have thought? They differentiate by context and hand signals, which I hadn't learned yet. Furthermore, what he actually said was four-ten, which means 40, but I didn't know how to say numbers above ten. Again I pulled out a small wad of bills and handed him four of the second smallest size. I thought that might be a safe guess at the price.

He started yelling. I stood there, confused and embarrassed. What had I done wrong?

A few people sensed that something interesting was going on so they crowded near to watch. In Mainland China in 1996, a major form of entertainment was gathering around accidents or fights, or a stupid white woman who didn't know how to buy mangoes.

Every few seconds several more people stopped to gawk and guffaw. Finally, about 40 people were standing around us, and they were all laughing at me.

The mango hawker then took out four orange/gray notes that were a little larger than the four I had given him. He waved them in my face. (It was 40 *kuai*—about five dollars.)

I couldn't believe the mangoes could be that expensive, especially since a head of broccoli had probably only cost five cents. Later I found out that mangoes were very expensive in Wuran. But at the time, I was sure he was cheating me, so I shouted at him most of the rest of my vocabulary: "*Bu, bu, bu*!" ("No, no, no!")

The whole crowd roared even louder. The hawker's face turned red and he yelled a whole stream of words I couldn't understand. This lasted for several minutes until I realized that I just needed to leave without the mangoes. As I walked away, the crowd was still laughing, and the hawker yelled at me all the way down the street.

I walked home as fast as I could, keeping my head down, trying not to make eye contact with anyone. We ate stir-fried broccoli, and peanut butter and jelly sandwiches that evening.

Later, in the middle of the night, I woke up. My heart was pounding and I was panting. Sweat was pouring off me. I couldn't stop thinking about my attempt to buy mangoes. I was going to have to go to the market every day to buy food unless I wanted my family to eat peanut butter and jelly the rest of our lives. But I couldn't do it! I started to sob, and as my sobbing grew louder and louder, Justin woke up beside me.

"What's wrong, Grace?"

Between sobs I gasped, "I can't go to the market! I can't get food for our family to eat. And we have to eat three times a day. *Three times every single day!* What am I going to do?"

"Don't worry about it. I'll do all the shopping and cooking. Just go back to sleep."

True to his word, Justin went to the market every day to shop, and he cooked our meals. This was in addition to language school, fathering our sons, dealing with the police, spending about eight hours a week on repairs in our apartment, and all the other responsibilities he handled to keep the family running. He never complained.

Meanwhile, in addition to studying Mandarin, housework, and parenting, I asked Peter to teach me the names of foods, denominations of money, weights and measures, and, of course, how to count higher than ten, so I could try to return to the market.

I prayed that the Lord would calm my fear because I didn't want Justin to keep pulling a double load.

I remembered a book I had read out of curiosity a few years earlier about phobias and how to get rid of them. It said that step by step you need to slowly accustom yourself to the situation you fear.

So a month after my first expedition to the market, I said to Justin, "How about if I go to the market with you? I won't buy anything; in fact, I won't even say a word. I just need to get used to being in the market." Walking along the market street with Justin, I was still afraid, but I didn't have a panic attack. I accompanied him every day for a month.

Then I told him, "I'll try to buy something this time in the market, but at the first sign of trouble, you step in and take over negotiations."

Every month I took over more of the bargaining. Gradually I calmed down and became confident, until finally, six months later, after a month of shopping alone, I caught myself smiling as I left the market street—I had had fun talking with the vendors!

Learning to function in a new country in a language I was just learning was traumatic and humiliating, but after a while, as I became more competent, my success and the friendships I was making filled me with pride and joy. But no matter how fluent I became in Mandarin, or how well I came to understand the culture, just about every single day in Asia, someone would say or do something I didn't understand, and I felt humiliated. But I got used to it.

Suffering small humiliations on a daily basis changes a person. It made me not care so much what people thought of me; it set me free to stand up for what I believe and go against the cultural currents even when people oppose me. It also enabled me to do gutsy, unpopular righteous acts in service to the Lord, no matter what the consequences. But it especially freed me to share the gospel, regardless if people look down on me or laugh at me.

THE FIGHT

1996, Wuran

Many nights during our first year in Mainland China, we would hear destruction on the street behind our apartment. Sheets of metal crashing. The sound of merchandise being thrown to the ground and tables overturned. We couldn't sleep with all the noise, so night after night we would look out our bedroom window onto a disturbing scene—about 50 old people were dismantling the tiny kiosks where during the day vendors sold small items like rubber bands, cheap snacks or bottles of water.

We couldn't figure out why the seniors were throwing the merchandise to the ground and destroying the kiosks, so later we asked our Chinese friend, Peter. He told us, "The communist government doesn't like the kiosks because the vendors are capitalists. So at night, while the vendors are asleep, the government orders work units of old people to dismantle them!"

The government was destroying the vendors' slim livelihood while they slept? I was quite sure these sellers were living hand to mouth.

When we walked down the street, we noticed little wooden handwritten signs jammed into the cracks of the curbs: "Carpenter from ___ Province," "Pipe fitter from ___ Province," "Plumber from ___ Province" ... Each province had the reputation for being the best at a certain skill. Next to each sign stood a sad, scruffy man who had traveled from his home province in the hope of being hired for a freelance job in this city of nine million. The men were that desperate for a few bucks.

One day, we saw a truck mowing down the signs! I was so angry—these men were just trying to feed their families, but the government of the so-called People's Republic of China was making it impossible for them to find work! At that time, there weren't any acceptable avenues to market skills and there were no job advertisements.

What was happening? Until recently, everyone in the country had been employed by government-owned enterprises, and everything was decided by central planning. But most of the government businesses were failing and the government was unwilling to keep propping them up. In the late 1990s, when we arrived in Mainland China, the communist government realized that socialism was bankrupting the economy, so they shut down the government enterprises that were money-drains, laying off much of the half-billion-strong workforce in just a few years' time!

Since the Communist Revolution, the Chinese people had always been provided with jobs, so they didn't know how to find work, and there were no jobs to be had anyway. They were desperate, and they had never seen what capitalism looked like. Many of the older newly unemployed never did figure out how to earn a living, so they just stayed home, and their families took care of them with what meager resources they had. The more enterprising ones made a guess at how a capitalist makes money and attempted to remake themselves in any way they could think of—selling rubber bands, water, cheap snacks or hiring out their skilled labor. But the government wasn't comfortable yet with the man on the street making money, so it was sabotaging their efforts.

Anger was building in the common people. They lost their jobs, then watched the government destroy any hope they had of earning a living. This rage spilled into the streets in public brawls and fist fights. When we first arrived in Mainland China, while walking down the street, we often saw fights suddenly break out right in front of us.

After several years, the policy of the government changed, as it realized that the people had to find work somehow in order to feed themselves. What a revelation! Then the country shifted its slogan to "Socialism with Chinese Characteristics," which meant mostly capitalist but with tight political control. Since the government was willing to accept capitalism in practice, even if not in name, after that the people were able to find employment, so the anger calmed down and we didn't see as much fighting in the streets.

§§§

But one of the first fights we saw in Mainland China could have seriously harmed me because I acted to stop it.

One morning, three weeks after we moved to Wuran, I was biking to language school on the dirt road that led from our apartment complex to the main thoroughfare. Garbage and bricks were strewn on both sides of the road. I had to weave to avoid the basketball-sized potholes.

Suddenly a small yellow van-taxi screeched to a stop a dozen feet ahead of me and ten men and women jumped out the back, all of them yelling at each other. They faced off in groups of twos and threes.

I immediately stopped my bike. Then my breath caught as I watched everyone grab bricks from the side of the road and wave them above their heads at their opponents.

I hate violence—whether against people, cats or snakes—and I've risked my life to save each of them when they were being attacked. When I see violence against a living being, I completely forget my own safety.

Seeing how brutal this fight might become, my mind was racing, I wanted to try to stop it before anyone got killed, but I didn't know how. I was quite sure that if I interfered by trying to calm them down it would only inflame the situation. Furthermore, at that time I could only speak a few words of Mandarin.

So I did the only thing I could think of. I dismounted and quickly walked over to the nearest group of two men. They were shouting, gesticulating wildly, and shaking their bricks over their heads at each other. I stood between them, facing one with my back to the other. I knew that they might bash my brain in, if only accidentally. I didn't say a word.

Lord, please keep these people from killing each other! And keep them from killing me!

At first the two men didn't notice me, they were so intent on their argument. But suddenly, the man in front of me focused in on me and his jaw dropped. He didn't know what to do. How was he supposed to continue the fight with a white woman standing between him and his enemy? He put his brick down on the ground and looked ashamed. Then the man behind me dropped his brick.

I breathed a sigh of relief. This was just the effect I was hoping to have.

The three of us stood there, silent. Then a woman in a group of three to my right looked over at me and put her brick down. Her two opponents did the same.

Everyone was becoming quiet and staring at me. Finally, the last two groups of people also laid their bricks down, that is, all except for one man.

Someone had run to tell a security guard, who walked up right then. In true Chinese communist fashion, he calmly lectured them at length.

But I kept watching the man with the brick. He had never laid it down, but was still holding it at his side, ready. And he still looked angry.

The security guard was standing on my left. I tugged on his sleeve. He was annoyed at my interruption of his lecture and ignored me. I tugged again. Finally, he turned toward me, irritated. I didn't know how to say the word "brick," so pointing at the brick, I used two words of my extremely limited vocabulary, "*Ta you! Ta you!*" ("He has! He has!")

The guard looked at the brick in the man's hand and spoke to him. The man put the brick down.

The tightness in my back started to ease. Everyone was safe. *Thank you, Lord.*

Another day in China.

NOWHERE IS SAFE

1996, Wuran

Twelve-year-old Nigel raced up the stairs to our apartment and slammed the door behind him. His eyes were wide as he tried to catch his breath. "Mom, quick, the police are on the third floor ransacking an apartment. I think they might be coming here!"

"Slow down," I said. "What's going on?"

"You know the Mabeline who lives two floors down, the Singaporean guy? Well, the police are raiding his apartment. We need to be ready! They might come here next!" Nigel said between gasps. *Mabeline* was our family code word for missionary. Justin and Adam weren't home, so it was just the two of us.

I sprang into action and dug up the contraband Christian material we had hidden in the apartment. We had only lived in Mainland China for a few months, and we hadn't thought the police would go so far as to raid our home. Now that it looked like a real possibility, I feared the materials were not hidden well enough. Where could I put it?

I opened the bedroom door and looked around but couldn't see a good hiding place. Then I looked in the boys' room. No safe place there. Finally, the storage closet. Our coats! Maybe they won't look in the sleeves of our coats. I stuffed Christian teaching materials down the sleeves of each coat.

A basket! Could I hang a basket out the window? They wouldn't see it from inside. I could stuff that with materials.

After everything was hidden, I started pacing the floor, waiting. *Lord, please protect us!*

Finally, I couldn't stand it any longer. "Nigel, what if you and I pretend to go out for ice cream? We'd pass by the Singaporean's apartment, and we could glance in to see what's going on."

Nigel agreed, and we walked down the stairs, pretending to chat about buying ice cream. The door to the Singaporean's apartment was wide open and we saw six men with the cold-blooded, powerful bearing of communist policemen talking inside. They were the kind who could crush you under the iron boot of Marxism. A chill went down my spine.

We stayed away about ten minutes. When we returned, laughing and talking to keep up the ruse, the Singaporean's apartment was quiet, and the door was shut. Everything looked back to normal. We breathed a sigh of relief, but we weren't sure what we'd find at our apartment.

After we climbed two more flights, we found our home locked and quiet. The police hadn't come to our apartment. This had been a targeted raid.

The next day a coworker of the Singaporean stopped me on the street. She glanced around to make sure no one could hear, then whispered, "Do you know what happened last night? The police came to the Singaporean's apartment and raided it!"

"Yes, we know. Did they take anything?"

"Yeah. The real loss is that they took his computer. There were a lot of emails to other China ministries on that computer, which could put them in danger. But the strange thing is, the police rifled through the Singaporean's clothes and took a few pieces. They even went through his underwear! Apparently, he arranges his underpants very carefully," she grinned. "And they took only a few pairs from the center!"

I cringed. "Wow, that's really too bad about his ministry contacts. We'll pray. I hope those ministries will be OK. And what was that about the police going through his underwear?"

We both agreed it was a power play. The police were trying to intimidate the Singaporean: "We can even go through your most intimate apparel," their actions said.

We don't know why the police didn't kick the Singaporean out of the country and we don't know how many of his contacts were compromised. But after that police raid, the private space of our home didn't feel so private anymore. We were also more careful where we hid our Christian contraband after that, even to the point of asking a friend to store Christian materials one time when it looked like the police might raid our home.

TRYING TO ARRIVE

1997-1999, Wuran

"Get out! Get out of my car!" the driver of the car we had rented shouted in Mandarin at Justin, Nigel (14), Adam (12), and me. But where were we supposed to go? He was kicking us out on the side of the freeway in a desolate, uninhabited place.

We had hired this car and driver to take us from Wuran to Huangdi for dental appointments, a two-and-a-half-hour drive—there weren't any qualified dentists in our city of nine million. Tolls were included in the price, but the driver now decided that he didn't want to pay the toll after all. Justin argued with him that he had already agreed to pay it, but "Get out!" was his only response.

How were we supposed to make our appointments? And how long would we be stuck in this barren place at the side of the road?

Looking around, I spotted an empty taxi coming in our direction along the freeway. I raced to the shoulder of the highway and stuck out my hand to wave him down.

"Could you take us to this address in Huangdi?" I asked in Mandarin, as I held out the business card of the dentist.

But just as he was looking at the card, our previous driver ran over and shouted to him, "These people owe me money! Don't take them!"

The taxi sped off! I yelled after it, "We don't owe him any money!" But the Chinese drivers were showing solidarity with each other.

How had we landed in this predicament? Originally, we had planned to take a *bus* from Wuran to Huangdi. As we were about to enter the bus station, a tall, well-dressed man offered to drive us in an expensive black sedan for 200 RMB.[16]

"Does the price include tolls and gas?" Justin asked in Mandarin. Justin is very careful and doesn't like to be cheated.

"Yes, of course."

I looked at the car longingly. The bus wasn't very comfortable or convenient. This car would be so much more luxurious and relaxing than the bus, and would make the trip easier. The price was about the same as bus tickets for the four of us, so we took the black sedan.

Everything was peaceful until the driver went through the toll booth and insisted we pay the toll, which Justin refused to pay as per our agreement.

So he pulled off to the right and shouted at us to get out. Then our driver parked and walked over to a group of about ten drivers and started shooting the breeze with them.

After I was unsuccessful in hiring the passing taxi, I looked at my watch. It was only an hour and a half until our dental appointments.

Lord, here we are in the middle of nowhere. Please help us find a way out of here and help us make it to our appointments.

Nigel looked around. "Look, there's a police station. For sure they'll help us!"

The four of us walked into the small cement block building. Five policemen were standing in a circle engaged in conversation. I was scared to talk with them and Justin doesn't like confrontations, so Nigel walked over to them. "We have a problem with our driver," he began in Mandarin. After glancing at us, the group of policemen ostentatiously turned their backs on us. They didn't want to hear a complaint from an American against a fellow Chinese.

Discouraged, we trudged out of the police station. No help there.

---

[16] RMB (renminbi) is the name of Chinese currency.

In the area between the door of the police station and the clump of laughing drivers, the four of us huddled together.

Justin said, "When we were in the car, I overheard the driver talking to someone on the phone. It seemed like it was his boss. From the way our driver was so solicitous and obsequious, the guy on the other end was probably a very high official. The driver told him that he would have the car back in Huangdi soon."

"That's our hope then," I said, feeling brighter. "He has a time limit. He can't stay here forever. He's trying to make a little extra money by ferrying us in his boss' car that he has to bring to Huangdi anyway. We'll wait him out. We could wait 45 minutes before we'll be late for the dentist. So the plan is this—if his deadline comes before ours, then he'll find a way to take us because he wants our 200 RMB for the trip. If our deadline comes before his, then we'll pay him the toll and be on our way."

Now that we had a plan, we all relaxed and started laughing and joking.

Finally, after another 20 minutes, the driver looked at his watch and signaled for us to join the drivers. He sneered and asked in Mandarin, "What country are you from?"

"America."

"Since America is such a poverty-stricken nation that her citizens can't even afford to pay a toll, out of the goodness of my heart, to help some poor Americans, I'll take you in my car and even pay the toll myself."

We tried not to laugh. He didn't believe a word he was saying about America—many Chinese want to immigrate to America, and most Chinese love America, that is, except when their communist government tells them not to. He was just using this put-down of America to try to save face for changing his mind. But it was just as we hoped—he had run out of time and he wanted our money.

We got in the car and sailed off again. Justin was in the front seat and I was in the back with the boys.

Nigel spoke up. "I had a dispute with a cab driver once and after I got out of the taxi, he tried to run me over!"

I gulped. "Then we need to handle this very carefully when we get out so we'll be safe." I was whispering just in case our driver could understand English. "Justin, give me all the small bills you have."

Surreptitiously, Justin began passing bills to the back seat. I leaned forward so the driver wouldn't see me counting our accumulated bills.

"Enough! I've got the 200 RMB!" I whispered. "When we arrive, you three get out of the car and Justin, get the boys as far away from the car as you can. Since I'm a woman I should be safer—he'll be less likely to beat me up. Only after you're some distance from the car will I hand him this stack of small bills and then get away myself while he's counting them. Hopefully we'll all be gone by the time he's finished counting and realizes I only gave him what we originally agreed on—200 RMB."

The plan worked. *Thank you, Lord!* But we always took the uncomfortable, inconvenient bus after that. It was more relaxing.

§§§

One day I was traveling alone by bus to Huangdi to see a doctor. When I got off the bus, I waved down a taxi to take me to the clinic.

Sitting in the front seat, about ten minutes into the ride I realized that he wasn't taking me to the clinic at all—in fact, he was taking me *out of the city to the countryside!*

Why did he want to take me to the countryside?

Then I remembered the story an American friend told me about a taxi he had taken from Huangdi to Wuran. His taxi had also driven him *out to the countryside* and demanded 600 RMB from him. He didn't have that much money on him, and it was three times what he had originally agreed to pay. The driver refused to take him home until he paid up, and where the driver had brought him in the countryside, there were no other buses or taxis he could take to get back on a main road to find his way home. He was stuck! Finally, the only thing our friend could think to do was offer to give the driver the money if he would take him to an ATM. It was an expensive ride, but at least he made it safely home.

But sitting in my taxi, heading out to the countryside, I was extra scared because I'm a woman. Although China usually *feels* safe in this way, it actually isn't that safe. I've had repeated difficulty with men in

China. So why was this driver taking me out to the countryside? Money or sex?

I looked around. How fast were we going? Could I open the car door and jump out without hurting myself? I didn't think so.

Lord, keep me safe! Give me an idea what to do!

I racked my brain for possible scenarios and escape options. Finally, I sweetly asked the driver in Mandarin, "Where are we going?"

The driver didn't answer me. Instead, he did the strangest thing—immediately, he made a U-turn, headed back into the city, and dropped me off at the clinic!

I breathed a sigh of relief. *Thank you, Lord, you saved me!*

PREDATOR

2000, Wuran
(This story is continued from "Jesus, the Sorcerer?")

Nate and Kathy were not only growing in the Lord, but about six weeks after they came to faith, one of Kathy's friends, Amy, wanted to start studying the Bible with Kathy. I was so excited. Even though we had only lived in Mainland China for three years, I might soon become a spiritual grandma!

But before I could teach Kathy how to study the Bible with Amy, disaster struck.

Our family was planning to travel for six weeks during the Spring Festival (Chinese New Year), and for the time we'd be gone, Justin asked Allen, our American mission leader, to disciple Nate and Kathy.

Shortly after we returned in February, before I had a chance to reconnect with Nate and Kathy, I got a call from Allen late one afternoon. "I need to talk to you about Kathy. Could we meet at the noodle shop for supper?"

When I walked into the noodle shop from the cold evening, welcome steam was rising from the fragrant vats of chicken broth. I looked around and spotted Allen waiting for me.

After ordering our noodles, we sat at one side of a large, round Formica® table to eat. I wrapped my hands around the bowl to warm them.

Allen turned to me, "Kathy and I fell in love!"

I froze—Allen was married with two kids, and his wife was very pregnant with their third! And this was Kathy who just six weeks before had been so excited about following the Lord. I felt even more repulsed because I could tell Allen wasn't upset about the affair. In fact, he seemed proud that a beautiful, 20-year-old woman was in love with him, a married man in his late 20s.

He continued while I looked at him in disgust. "I hired her to make and sell donuts at the donut shop I own, but I've given up managing the shop in order to stay away from her. I've decided not to continue the relationship, and I'm telling you because I'd like you to comfort Kathy. I plan to stay with my wife."

I was confused. Ostensibly, Allen was making a good decision, but something wasn't right—instead of remorse, he was animated and full of excitement.

In fact, at this moment he wasn't even treating *me* right. He kept smirking at me in a flirty way like he was a naughty boy taking a married woman out on a date. I was about 15 years older than he was, and I knew he wasn't attracted to me.

I wished I hadn't met with him alone. That was really dumb. Justin could have dealt with him in a masculine way, man-to-man.

Allen was a tall Scandinavian American who had a ready laugh and an incisive, calm way of seeing a problem through to its solution. A number of years ago he had moved his family to China in order to start small businesses. And, with his cool, intelligent mind, he was good at it, even with all the complications of running a business in China.

In many ways, he was a really nice guy. At the request of a mutual friend, he and his wife, Alethia, had opened their home to us almost four years earlier. We slept in the loft of their apartment while we checked out Wuran to see if we could move there. All Allen asked was that we bring a box of cold cereal from America for Alethia because it wasn't available in China, and she missed it so much.

Allen had been our mission leader for a little over half a year. He had never been a missionary before, and I found out later he didn't even spend time reading the Bible or praying. How had he been placed in a position of mission leadership? Our mission agency had stopped looking for people to fill positions of leadership based on their ministry experience and godly walk with the Lord; the current trend was toward people whose only qualification was that they were businessmen. It was a recipe for disaster.

Shortly after Allen came to the position, he and I had a long conversation during which he laughed about sin. I came home shaken, and told Justin that our new mission leader didn't hate sin.

And here he was now telling me to "comfort" a Chinese woman I had led to the Lord because he, our married mission leader, was breaking up with her!

I went home and talked it over with Justin, then I invited Kathy to come over the next day.

When she arrived, all bundled up, her face looked strained and she could hardly smile. I greeted her warmly, but she seemed distant.

She told me, "I only had a little feeling for Allen at first, and decided not to feed it or act on it because I knew it was wrong since he's married. But after he started to pursue me, I had more and more feelings for him. And even though he told you that our relationship is over, he's still calling me every day!"

I said, "Kathy, you need to stop having any contact with him whatsoever." I showed her what the Scriptures say about sexual immorality, and how we should flee from it (I Corinthians 6:18). Then I explained the slippery slope of how an affair with a married man develops and the damage it causes. Her face was set like stone; I couldn't get through.

Then I said, "This is really hurting Allen's wife, Alethia." At that, her face softened and she became pensive because she personally knew Alethia and liked her. Chinese people are very interpersonal, and often interpersonal reasons are more convincing to them than moral reasons.

The next day Kathy told Allen she didn't want him to call her anymore. When Allen asked why, she said because it hurts Alethia. But when relating this conversation with Allen, Kathy told me that Allen said that wasn't true, that Alethia wasn't being hurt by the affair.

Whatever the truth was, it meant I couldn't use the pain it was causing Alethia to talk sense into Kathy. It thwarted my attempts to encourage them to end the relationship and restore the marriage.

Then Kathy said to me, "So Allen told me that I hadn't convinced him, and he would continue to call me." Kathy wasn't strong enough to take a stand, not just because she was a new believer and in love with him, but because young unmarried Chinese women in the 1990s in our area didn't usually stand up to men. Also, her own resolve had crumbled because she now believed the affair wasn't hurting Alethia.

After Kathy left, I couldn't stop crying. This was the woman who had told me a few months ago that she wanted to read the whole Bible so she could obey everything the Lord wanted. Now she didn't seem to care what the Bible said. Because she wasn't fleeing from temptation, she kept getting dragged further and further into sin (James 1:14-15). And her heart was being hardened by the deceitfulness of sin (Hebrews 3:13).

Shortly afterward, Justin and I found out that Allen inexplicably broke off the relationship with Kathy. We breathed a sigh of relief.

But Kathy stopped meeting with me because Allen told her to have nothing to do with me. It seems he had a pernicious, manipulative influence on her, even when they were not together.

For over a month we thought the affair was over, until Nate, Kathy's former boyfriend, came over for a visit. We sat on the couch in the room upstairs with the chestnut vaulted ceiling. In a pained voice he told me, "I think something's going on between Allen and Kathy again. Can you help?"

My throat tightened. Nate was such a sweet, gentle guy, but he looked like he'd been to hell and back. And it was obvious he was still in love with Kathy—when he talked about her, his voice softened.

My heart ached for him. "I'm so sorry, Nate. Thanks for letting me know. I'll see if I can help."

Nate still liked me, that was obvious, but there was also a coolness in him toward me, now that a married "Christian" man we had introduced to him had stolen the love of his life. I'm sure he also questioned whether the Christian faith was as good as he had thought.

I was able to remain calm during our visit, but after he left, I raged around the apartment, shouting at an imaginary Allen.

Justin and I decided we needed to meet with Allen the next day. Oh, did we hope Nate wasn't right!

That evening, first, we prayed fervently for me. If I was still consumed with anger when Allen came over, I would say all the wrong things. *Lord, please calm me down and give me your love for this horrible man.* Then we prayed for wisdom to know what to say, and finally we begged the Lord to help the four of them.

By the time Allen showed up at our apartment at nine the next morning, the Lord had answered our first prayer—I was no longer raging. I was sad and calm.

I didn't take him upstairs to the room with the chestnut vaulted ceiling—that was reserved for people I liked. We sat downstairs in the living room.

After serving him coffee, asking about his wife's pregnancy and his business, I said, "Are you seeing Kathy again?"

He started by accusing *us*. "You know, *you* were the ones who introduced me to Kathy. I wouldn't have even known her if it weren't for *you* ..."

After he rabbit-trailed for ten minutes, I asked again, "Are you seeing Kathy?"

"Of course. I have to see her on occasion, she works at my donut shop." What kind of nonsense was this? He knew what I meant. Also, hadn't he told me a month ago that he had given up managing the shop so he could stay away from her?

He continued, "Does your question include phone calls? How many phone calls do you consider acceptable?" He smirked. Then he went into great length about every phone call he had made to her for business purposes. He concluded with, "So you must not be implying that phone calls are a problem."

He was muddying everything so much it was clear to me he was hiding that their relationship had resumed. So, 45 minutes into his twisted monologue, I rephrased my question. "Have you started up your romantic relationship with Kathy again?" Living in a communist country with all its lies, I had learned to press for the truth when I needed to.

His eyes narrowed in on me. "Have you talked with Nate and Kathy about sex? *You* led them to the Lord. You must have talked with them about sex. That was *your* responsibility."

My breath caught and I swallowed hard.

He continued his attack. "Do you even know how far Nate and Kathy are going?"

He was implying that Nate and Kathy were sleeping together, and he blamed me if they were. But that wasn't the issue here. And furthermore, it was Allen who was Kathy's boyfriend now, not Nate.

I didn't say much about his accusations because self-doubt was creeping in. Had I discipled Nate and Kathy as well as I should have? When I disciple someone, I don't load them down with laws from the Bible. Discipling, as with everything else in my life, is more organic and relational. But had I said enough about topics like sex?

Allen probably saw that he had scored some self-doubt in me, so he bulldozed ahead, accusing me of everything he could imagine. I was reeling by the time he was finished. But this meeting wasn't about me. It was about Allen. He was trying to shift the blame.

§§§

By now, Justin was fatigued, his eyes glazed over and he was no longer registering what was said. His Southern upbringing, which was kind and gentle and nonargumentative, had kept him quiet for much of the conversation. But I come from New York, where we love a friendly debate. So I had the New York stamina to pursue the truth in this conversation with Allen for as long as necessary.

Since truth usually prevails, I listened closely for hints of it.

But I don't know why we let Allen talk so long. After he had detoured, accused, and obfuscated for *seven hours*, finally I suggested we go out for a bite to eat. I was famished. This time when we walked into the restaurant, I didn't even notice the aromas emanating from the kitchen I was so upset.

After we sat down to eat, Allen relaxed a little and made a slip. He said, "Kathy and I haven't had physical contact."

I hadn't even asked about physical contact because I was assuming the relationship wasn't sexual. After all, he was our mission leader.

Naïve me. But his very denial convinced me they were involved sexually, so I asked him point blank, "Have you and Kathy had sexual contact?"

When I asked that question, Justin jarred up and started to listen.

Allen gave the strangest reply. "My wife would have to be present for me to answer that."

How warped can it get?

After that, Allen went into full rebellion mode. "I'm going to tell Kathy to see me tonight. She does whatever I tell her to do." Our hearts sank. We were quite sure he was going to sleep with her that night just to spite us! We begged him to repent.

When Allen left, Justin and I were exhausted. After returning home, we held each other, feeling forlorn. We grieved for Allen, Alethia, Kathy, and Nate. Then I cried for myself. Allen had been so mean to me. "Am I really that bad?" I asked Justin.

We had confronted Allen because Nate had asked us to help; we also knew it was the right thing to do and it would be hard. But we hadn't expected that it would hurt me so badly.

After I wiped my tears, Justin and I snuggled together on the sofa, and Justin opened the Bible to Matthew 18:15-17: "If your brother or sister sins, go and point out their fault, just between the two of you. If they listen to you, you have won them over. But if they will not listen, take one or two others along, so that 'every matter may be established by the testimony of two or three witnesses.' If they still refuse to listen, tell it to the church; and if they refuse to listen even to the church, treat them as you would a pagan or a tax collector."

I responded, "The main purpose in confronting someone is to bring about repentance, but this passage is also emphasizing that it's important to separate the church from those who claim to be godly Christians if they refuse to repent. It's a scary thing to do."

Then we looked at Galatians 6:1: "Brothers and sisters, if someone is caught in a sin, you who live by the Spirit should restore that person gently. But watch yourselves, or you also may be tempted."

"So we need to be gentle and humble," I said, "and make sure we don't think we're better than Allen because we could fall, too."

Finally, we read I Corinthians 5:11-13: "You must not associate with anyone who claims to be a brother or a sister but is sexually immoral, … Do not even eat with such people. What business is it of mine to judge those outside the church? Are you not to judge those inside? God will judge those outside. 'Expel the wicked person from among you.'"

Justin said, "Again, one of the goals is the purity of the church." He looked over at me, studying my face.

"I don't want to do this," I said. "Do we really need to go down this path?"

"We have to follow the Scriptures," Justin said.

I sighed with dread.

Justin continued, "Let's look at it carefully. In Matthew 18:15-16, it says to show him his fault just between the two of you. We just did that, and I think the two of us would be viewed as one since we're married. It says that if he won't listen to you, you need to confront him with a witness present so everything's clear and we haven't misunderstood the situation. So we need a witness. But other than the witness, we are not to tell anyone. Maybe we can help them come to repentance by following this. If we can, no one else will ever have to know."

After discussing it further, we decided on a witness—Bart, the mission leader above Allen. He was another mission leader who had merely been chosen for the position because he was a businessman—he had never been a missionary before becoming our mission leader, and he had some pretty serious shortcomings. But we were sure he would take adultery seriously. Justin set up a meeting for the next evening. We were nervous. Telling one mission leader that another mission leader is having an affair would leave us pretty open to accusation.

When we walked into his office the next evening, Bart had already set up chairs in a circle; I appreciated the symbolism of equality. After we sat down, we unburdened ourselves to him. We didn't know how he would react. But still, it was such a relief because we had been carrying this terrible burden alone for what felt like a very long time, even though it was only five weeks.

Bart looked pained while we told him. Then he stood up and started yelling what a degenerate Allen was.

He called Allen right away to ask him to come over to meet with the three of us right then. But Allen delayed the meeting for two days in order to break up with Kathy so he could say they had no relationship. That way he figured we couldn't take the next step according to Matthew 18.

When the four of us did meet, Allen was his old slippery self—dodging questions, and blaming me in order to divert attention from himself.

We had never heard him say clearly that he was sleeping with Kathy, but in order to follow the instructions of Matthew 18 it was important for us to know. Even aside from all his attacks, this was such an unpleasant thing to do. We personally didn't want to know the answer.

I felt a sense of dread in the core of my being, but finally I looked Allen full in the face and asked, "Have you slept with Kathy?"

He looked down and said, "Yes."

Bart was livid. "You slimeball, you!" he yelled. "How could you do this?"

Justin and I looked away. Then both of us started to weep. My weeping turned to wailing.

Finally, I looked over at Allen and said, "I feel so sorry for Kathy."

Allen looked at me defiantly. "Well, she can't be pregnant because we always protect ourselves." Then he continued, "And there's no problem as far as God is concerned, because each time, right after we make love, I always lead Kathy in asking God's forgiveness."

I stared at him with my mouth open. This was pretty warped. But it reminded me of something. Allen followed a particular tradition before he supposedly became a Christian. I knew the drill from knowing many in New York who followed the same tradition: sleep with someone, go to confession, say your punitive Hail Marys so you'll be forgiven, then sleep with that person again. But it wasn't Christian because there was no repentance from the heart and turning away from sin.

Allen concluded with, "I'm not sorry for what I did."

What do you do with this? He had broken up with her, but he was unrepentant.

After Allen left, Bart paced the floor, raging. "We have to kick him out of the mission. We are all in a lot of danger here. The Chinese government hates it when a foreign man sleeps with a Chinese woman. If they find out and question Allen, he might rat out the whole mission."

I spoke up. "I think it's better if you don't kick him out of the mission yet, but it would be good if we could get him to move back to America. As a mission, we don't actually have any control over him, but Allen might be confused and think we do. We may be able to use our perceived authority to get him to leave China. A lot of problems could be solved that way."

Then I added, "Also, Allen doesn't want us to follow what Matthew 18 tells us to do, so I suspect he's going to try to turn us against each other to distract us from dealing with his sin."

It took only two days for Allen to do just that. He called Bart and told him there was an urgent matter and Bart needed to come to his apartment right away. The emergency was that Allen supposedly knew some horrible things about me, and Bart needed to get Justin and me over to Allen's home *right then* so Allen could confront me with Bart as the witness.

Matthew 18 weaponized!

Thank God I had warned Bart, although he might have seen through that one even if I hadn't said anything. But he did remember my warning and refused to hear the dirt Allen had on me. He told Allen that if he had something against me he needed to confront Justin and me alone first, just as Matthew 18 says.

Thank God for Bart's spiritual wisdom and clarity about doing what the Scripture says. Following Scripture solves a lot of problems.

A few days later Allen did confront me in front of Justin, but it all fizzled. It was an accusation with no basis. In any case, his original intent had been to humiliate me in front of Bart. That way Bart would turn against me and we wouldn't be able to work together, but he hadn't succeeded.

Justin and I have noticed that even when both of us acted together, abusive people tend to target only me. It's always confused us. We figure abusers must have antennae for sensitive people because they know they get extra mileage out of hurting the sensitive ones. Of the two of us, I'm the one who most easily can be wounded. But although they can hurt me deeply, I don't bend. In fact, I become stronger in my resolve.

Allen's baseless accusation actually helped me. I began to see more clearly that all of his accusations came from ulterior motives, so after that I didn't take them as seriously. I stopped hurting so much, grew stronger and developed thicker skin. I matured.

But Allen became more and more depraved. Sin seemed to be turning his heart into a slimy mess.

Justin and Bart discussed what to do. They decided to study the Bible with Allen to see if they could help him come to repentance and turn to the Lord. I was so glad they took it over and it was out of my hands now.

In the meantime, the three of us would say nothing to anyone. If Allen would continue to stay away from Kathy, we wouldn't take it any farther, and no one else would know.

§§§

Not long after that, Kathy invited me to her family's home for dinner.

In all my time living in Hong Kong and China, I have never visited such a tiny, humble apartment. The whole family lived in a single nine-by-eight-foot room. It didn't have any kitchen or bathroom.

"Where do you cook? And where's your bathroom?" I asked in Mandarin.

Kathy's mom pointed out the door. "There's a burner down the hall; everyone shares it. And, of course, we use the communal bathroom."

Two bunk beds, each two-and-a-half feet wide, lined the side walls at the back, taking up almost two-thirds the length of the room, with a narrow walkway between. Her parents crammed a small, foldable rectangular table into the space between the last two feet of the beds, extending past the beds toward the door. On it they placed steaming dishes of delicious northern Chinese food with its thick sauces. The aromas of soy sauce, fish sauce, and pork mingled together.

Kathy and I sat on the beds facing each other with the table between us. Her mother and father sat at the table opposite each other on folding chairs at the end of the bunks.

Halfway through the meal, her mother said, "Isn't it great that Kathy and Allen are together!"

I nearly choked on my food. I looked across at Kathy, who kept her face expressionless. I suspected her mother didn't realize they weren't together anymore.

I blurted out, "But Allen's married!"

The mother smiled a contented smile. "That doesn't matter. Now Kathy will be able to immigrate to the U.S."

Was that what this was all about? An opportunity to immigrate to America to have a better life? Apparently, that was at least Kathy's mother's goal. And whoever was destroyed on the way was just inconsequential collateral damage.

I thought back to a chilling article I had read in a Chinese newspaper a year and a half earlier. The title in Chinese was, "How to Immigrate to the U.S." It said that for women the best way was to attract an American man living in China. "It doesn't matter if he's married because, of course, with your charms you will be able to draw him away from his wife! He will divorce her and marry you ..."

Who was the predator here? Allen? Kathy? Or Kathy's mother?

§§§

All through this, we were praying fervently for Allen. As far as Justin and Bart meeting with him, it all hobbled along with Allen not that interested in the Lord, but staying away from Kathy.

That is, until one day in May, about a month after their meetings started, as the fragrant cherry blossoms were beginning to fade—Allen told Bart that while on a business trip to the U.S. he had started calling Kathy again ...

THE WEEPING CHURCH

2000, Wuran
(This story is continued from "Predator")

When Bart told us that Allen had started up the affair again, we were sad but not surprised. Looking back it seemed inevitable, since, for the month of meeting with Justin and Bart, Allen had just been going through the motions without repenting.

Bart, Justin, and I decided that we needed to tell the elders about the affair so they could deal with it according to Matthew 18. Justin was an elder at the international fellowship, so he arranged for the three of us to meet with the other elders—Aaron, Brent, Daniel, and Jack—that very evening, a Friday.

I felt comfortable with most of these men, but when bringing a problem like this, we didn't know what response we were going to get. We were putting ourselves on the line again.

We sat around a foldable rectangular table, and with resignation told the elders everything that happened—how we had tried to bring both Allen and Kathy to repentance, but failed. Then we sat quietly, waiting.

At first the elders were completely silent. They looked tense and grieved. Then Brent spoke up, "We need to pray."

After an anguished prayer, Brent looked around at the other elders. "They have followed Matthew 18 exactly. I can't think of a way they could have followed it more closely." He opened his Bible and in a halting voice read out loud Matthew 18:15-17 and I Corinthians 5:9-13.

Then Brent continued, "According to these Scriptures there remains one more thing to be done, and it is what we, as elders, need to do. We have to confront Allen to see if we can encourage him to repent. If he won't, then we need to cast him out of the church." He sighed.

I shuttered—had it really come to this? We had tried so hard to bring Allen to repentance so the church wouldn't have to discipline him.

Then Aaron, who was a friend of Allen's, cried out, "But we can't do this! Think of how much it will hurt Alethia."

My breath caught.

The other elders stared Aaron down. "It's not *we* who would be hurting Alethia, it's *Allen* who's hurting her. We do need to follow Scripture and make a clear statement about his adultery."

Aaron nodded almost imperceptibly and mumbled, "Yes, we do need to do this."

Now that the elders were agreed, a tiny bit of hope welled up in me—would Allen repent after the elders confronted him? Maybe their spiritual authority and numbers would help to change his heart where we hadn't been able to.

I also breathed a sigh of relief. The elders believed us! They would stand behind us and pick up the baton themselves. I looked around at their faces as they all nodded in agreement. They were strong, godly men who weren't going to shy away from following a difficult passage of Scripture.

After a short discussion, they all agreed they needed to confront Allen *immediately*. They were afraid if they waited, Allen might skip town or even manage to move back to the States before they could confront him. They wanted to make a clear statement to Allen about his adultery in the hope that they could bring him to repentance.

"We mustn't call him first to make an appointment," Aaron said. "If we do that, he'll delay. Instead, we need to surprise him. In fact, let's go right now."

As one, we stood and quietly, pensively, walked over to Allen's red brick apartment building, and climbed the cement stairs to his apartment. Alethia opened the door and saw the seven of us crammed into the hallway and down the stairs. She looked uneasy.

"We've come to talk to Allen," Brent said.

Alethia looked behind her, and with some trepidation, said, "Allen, the elders are here to see you."

After we all crowded in and Alethia found chairs for us to sit on, Daniel explained why we had come. Alethia and Allen were sitting close together on the couch. She gently reached out and put her hand on Allen's knee.

Daniel asked, "Allen, are you willing to stand up in front of the congregation and confess what you've done?"

"Yes, of course," Allen replied brightly. "I would be glad to tell everyone about my relationship with Kathy." He looked proud.

Daniel was pleased and turned to Bart, Justin, and me. "Would that satisfy you?"

The three of us simultaneously rose up from our chairs and shouted, "No!" Daniel was startled. Bart spoke in a loud voice. "When he says 'confess,' he does not mean repent! He has skewed the meaning of I John 1:9 to mean that if he confesses what he's doing wrong, but doesn't repent, he will be forgiven by the Lord. He's ignoring the rest of Scripture, which calls for us to turn away from our sin. You need to ask him if he will repent and stop the affair with Kathy."

Daniel turned back to Allen. "Are you willing to repent and stop sleeping with Kathy?"

"Of course not!"

The elders were shocked and began talking to each other, infuriated. Brent yelled at Allen, "You are making a mockery of the church and of repentance!"

I leaned toward Justin and whispered, "That would split the church because a lot of the congregation would mistake his confession for repentance. Then if the elders kicked him out, many would oppose them."

Jack asked Allen, "But what about your marriage vow to Alethia?"

Allen smiled. "I haven't broken my vow to Alethia. I'll never leave her." Pretty slim marriage vow.

Meanwhile Alethia rubbed Allen's knee gently—he needed comforting.

Daniel said to Allen, "If you will not repent, then we have no choice. Two days from now during the Sunday service, we will announce to the fellowship that we are expelling you from the church. We want you to repent." His voice broke. "We do not want to do this! But if you don't repent, we will."

We got up to leave, and as Aaron was walking out the door he turned around, and with tears in his eyes he begged Allen, "Please repent. Anytime day or night between now and Sunday morning, if you are willing to repent, call one of us. We don't care what time it is—we will stop everything and talk with you. Please, please call us."

After we exited the apartment building, the elders decided to convene in one of their apartments to discuss the details of how to proceed. I asked if I could come, and they agreed.

Again, we sat around a foldable rectangular table; one of the elders opened a computer to record the decisions. "What's the subject of the sermon on Sunday?" Brent asked. After we heard the answer he said, "It seems like the sermon should be on this topic." After a pause he asked, "Who would like to preach about adultery on Sunday?" He looked around, but unsurprisingly no one volunteered. Then he said, "Actually, I'd like to give the sermon."

I was taken aback. Who would want to preach a sermon like that?

Then I asked, "You said you would kick him out of the church, but, because we can't let the Chinese government find out the names of who's attending, we have no membership roll. So how can someone be kicked out of the church when their name was never put on a church roll?"

Aaron looked at me fiercely, "We elders will stand shoulder to shoulder and bar his way if he tries to enter!"

Wow! These men were determined to see this through. And now especially Aaron, Allen's friend.

They began to craft what they would say to the congregation. They planned to tell it orally in a way that didn't clearly state what Allen had done.

I spoke up. "Please forgive me, I hope I'm not overstepping here."

They nodded and asked me to give input.

I said, "We want to discourage gossip. You do that by making the situation absolutely clear, without giving too much detail. First, it needs to be in writing projected on the front screen. That way no one will misunderstand. Also, we have many in the congregation from different countries for whom English is not their first language. The non-native English speakers especially need to be able to read it. Furthermore, you don't want anyone mishearing the name." I then imitated a well-meaning parishioner asking the person next to him if it was *Aaron* who had committed adultery because he hadn't heard the name clearly.

I continued, "Don't say something like 'inappropriate behavior.' People may suspect it was malfeasance in his business dealings. If people don't know exactly what the problem is, they'll start guessing and gossiping. Tell them it's because of adultery, but don't go into detail. That's the best way to quell gossip in people who don't want to gossip." They took my suggestions.

We adjourned for the night, and each of us prayed fervently all weekend that Allen would repent. It was a tense weekend, but Allen never did call the elders. Instead, we heard wind of strange comments he was making against the church and the elders.

The next time I saw the elders was Sunday morning when we walked into the old-fashioned, shabby, cinema-style auditorium that the fellowship rented every Sunday for our services. We nodded at each other and smiled sadly. The elders, Bart, Justin, and I were the only ones who knew what was coming.

Brent spoke from two Bible passages—Genesis 39 where Joseph fled from the advances of Potiphar's wife, and II Samuel 11 where David committed adultery with Bathsheba, Uriah's wife. In his comparison, he pointed out that the main difference between the two was that Joseph fled temptation, but David didn't flee. Instead, David ran toward temptation.

Then he told a heart-wrenching story from his own life. You could feel the anguish beneath his words as he spoke. "In America, there is a woman who is determined to sleep with me. I kept moving from state to state to avoid her, but no matter what state I moved to, she would hunt me down and then surprise me by showing up at my door. One night she actually got into my apartment and wouldn't leave, so I had to flee my own apartment! Now that I'm married, when we're in America, she still shows up at my door. It's actually safer for us to live in China.

"Sadly, we need to tell you about someone who didn't flee temptation, whom the elders have decided to kick out of the fellowship because he refuses to repent. We are acting according to Matthew 18 and I Corinthians 5." Then he read those passages.

When the announcement about Allen was projected up on the screen, I heard gasps and groans throughout the auditorium.

Then a man in the congregation stood up, and in a voice full of sorrow cried out, "We want to pray! We want to pray! We need to pray for Allen, Alethia, and the woman. We need to pray for all of the marriages here. There are so many temptations to the marriages here in China. We must never stop praying for the marriages in this fellowship to be strong."

Spontaneously, with no direction from the elders, we broke into small groups to pour out our hearts to the Lord. Many were weeping.

What a godly fellowship!

§§§

The elders did have to deal with some fallout from a few people who complained that the affair should have been brought to the church as a whole for a decision and shouldn't have just been decided by the elders. Practically, that would have been very difficult because many unbelievers attended the fellowship and we had no membership, and also because Allen was so slippery. I don't know what the elders said to those people, but their complaint seemed to die down.

Aaron's wife stopped me on the street a few weeks after Allen was put out of the fellowship and told me that Alethia had forgiven *me*! It was shocking how twisted everything still was.

Allen went on to divorce Alethia and within a month he had married Kathy. They moved to America, so Kathy's mother got her wish. Allen continued to be snide—making fun of the church and the

Christian faith.

But I have heard that Kathy has returned to the Lord. I still pray for the four of them.

Shortly after Allen was expelled from the international fellowship, a friend of mine from the fellowship told me, “When I was young my father had an affair and it destroyed our family. If only the elders in my childhood church had been strong and done what these elders did, it would have saved our family. But instead, they took the easy way out and didn’t follow Scripture. They just ignored the problem.”

Many African men were studying medicine in the city of Wuran, but they couldn’t bring their wives and families with them to China. One of these men, who attended our fellowship, was having an affair with a Swiss woman who was also living in Wuran. He was so convicted after the elders took such a strong stand on adultery that he broke up with his Swiss lover. He made an international call to his wife in Africa and confessed the affair to her. The marriage was touch and go for a while, but eventually his wife found it in her heart to forgive him and their marriage was restored.

The church was being purified.

ENTANGLEMENTS

2001-2002, Wuran

Into the tiny tea room of her apartment where I was seated, Old Gai carried a wooden tray loaded with an antique clay tea set and several carafes of hot water. Both the squat, round teapot, and the cups, each cup the size of a few thimbles, were inscribed with the flourishes of beautiful Chinese calligraphy from days gone by.

With hardly a word, she began the tea ceremony. Her movements were executed with ancient tradition—the flourishes of her arms and hands as she rinsed the tea with boiling water, then steeped it for a precise number of seconds with fresh boiling water; the dramatic rise of her elbows as she poured the tea into our cups, an earthy and bitter aroma filling the room. I had never experienced the tea ceremony before, and I was intrigued with this ancient aspect of Chinese culture.

Old Gai and I had met just a week before, while I was taking my daily walk through the housing complex. She was about 60 years old. I was anxious to make more Chinese friends, so when she invited me to her home for the tea ceremony, I jumped at the opportunity. After that first memorable experience, she invited me over for tea every week. I felt like I was drinking deeply of the culture.

One day when I arrived she was exhausted, and she explained to me in Mandarin why she was so tired. "My granddaughter had a life-threatening illness. So I built up my *qi* [life energy force] through meditation and exercise. When my *qi* was strong enough, I gave it to my granddaughter, and it healed her. Now I don't have much *qi* left, so I'm very weak."

What she had just described was a Buddhist healing with its zero sum view of the world—Old Gai had to lose life energy in order for her granddaughter to gain life energy and be healed. Not like Christian healings, which spring from the inexhaustible outpouring of God's power and generosity—no one has to lose for someone else to gain.

After her disclosure, I asked about her Buddhist faith. I hoped eventually I would have the opportunity to direct the conversation toward Jesus. But she stopped me—she was unwilling to talk about anything of substance.

In fact, other than that one disclosure, our friendship didn't seem to progress normally. She wouldn't tell me anything else that was personal, and whenever I tried to veer off into personal topics, even about myself, she shut me down. All I was allowed to talk about was the tea ceremony. The relationship gradually became boring.

Then one morning, after we'd known each other a month, she located me practicing Tai Chi Sword Form with a couple of Chinese friends in an out-of-the-way grassy section of the housing complex. She pulled me aside and said, "I want you to teach English once a week to the daughter of my landlord."

I tensed up. People were always asking us to teach English, and if I taught everyone who asked, that's all I would spend my time doing. I graciously declined.

She turned around and stomped off, without so much as saying "goodbye." That was not only the end of the tea ceremonies, that was the last time I ever saw her. I was sad because I realized then that from the beginning the whole purpose of our supposed friendship had been to groom me for a favor—she had been performing the tea ceremony so I would be obligated to return a favor.

I had not been making a friend; I had been developing an obligation.

Not long after we moved to Mainland China, Justin and I realized that paying back favors was the basis of a lot of relationships, but these relationships only had a pretense of friendship. As soon as we figured the system out, we decided we would never participate. We wouldn't consider that we owed anyone anything, no matter what they had done for us or what they thought we owed them. It was countercultural, but we knew that if we got sucked into the *guanxi* system of returned favors, not only would it consume all our time, but it would never produce any real relationships or ministry. Our only value to our Chinese "friend" would be what they could get out of us.

Marxism, as it is practiced, is based on power. It's very difficult to get anything done in a communist country without cozying up to a powerful person and doing them favors so they will help or protect you. There's no equal opportunity under law; no justice, only power. This has seeped pervasively into everyday relationships in Mainland China where you do favors for someone so they will help you with a need.

Shortly after Old Gai stopped pretending to be my friend, I met another woman in our housing complex, Mrs. Liu. She was in her late 40s, very plump, and all dolled up. She also couldn't speak any English, and she was delighted to meet an American who could speak Mandarin. The first day we met, she invited me over for lunch. She wouldn't accept any invites from me, and after that first visit, every week she asked me over and cooked lunch for me. But once again I felt like there was something wrong with this "friendship." It wasn't as thin as the other relationship, but she was quite crass and finally she told me a crude story about her son. About the time I decided I didn't want to continue this "friendship," a month after we met, she asked me for a favor.

"My son overstayed his U.S. visa. I want you to call the American Embassy for me and straighten it out!"

"But I don't have those kinds of connections or that much influence," I replied.

"Of course you do! You're American. It's your embassy, after all!"

So this was payback time; I should have seen it coming. I made a phone call or two for her, but unsurprisingly, I got nowhere.

That was the last time I saw her, too. She had pretended to be friends with me because all along she had had an agenda—cozy up to an American so her son's visa problem would be solved.

My Chinese friends who really were my friends shared their hearts with me, and when they needed a favor, they usually waited a long time after an intimate friendship had developed before they asked. It didn't feel like payback—it felt like friendship. Furthermore, I could refuse a favor and they wouldn't walk out on me.

But the payback time that really scared me was actually orchestrated out of kindness, supposedly for my benefit, by a woman named Doris who truly was my friend.[17] Doris was a Buddhist woman whom I took walks with several times a week. She enjoyed trying to solve problems for me in out-of-the-box ways. One December when I was upset because I couldn't find a Christmas tree to buy, she told me in Mandarin, "That's no problem at all. Just chop down one of the beautiful trees planted in the gated upscale housing estate down the street!" When I objected because the guards at the gate would catch me, she said, "You do have to be careful. You'll have to do it at night so you can sneak it past the guards!"

Then she tried to help me solve a serious problem in a way that was even more dangerous for me.

The two of us often talked about Buddhist philosophy and after a while I began comparing it with Jesus' teachings. One day she looked at me with fear in her eyes. "I know what you're up to! And you're going to need protection! When the government catches you sharing about Jesus, you're going to need someone powerful who can keep you safe. I know just the man. He's the former mayor of Wuran, and he's my close friend. I'll work it out for you."

A few days later she was all excited when we went for our walk. "Come over to my home for dinner on Friday. I've invited the former mayor over. Make sure you dress up real pretty! Do you have a dress you could wear? And wear red!" (Red is the Chinese festive color.)

At home I told Justin, "I'm supposed to meet the former mayor of Wuran, and Doris wants me to dress up in red for it. I don't know what the plan is, but I don't feel comfortable—there's something fishy about

[17] This is the Doris from "Christianity Through the Eyes of a Buddhist" in *Dragon Ride*.

me meeting him. Also, we've always tried to keep a low profile because of our work. Meeting one of the most powerful men in Wuran doesn't fit with that low profile."

When I arrived at Doris' home, wearing red, the former mayor was already sitting in an easy chair. He looked about 65 years old, and there was nothing special about his appearance, except that he did exude a little power and assured confidence. Doris sat me next to him. I was getting more nervous.

Doris, her husband, and the former mayor kept chatting about all sorts of subjects in Mandarin, and I tried not to participate in the conversation. Then Doris' husband began railing against the Communist Party, the Chinese government, and the leaders of the country. I panicked. This was the former mayor he was talking to!

Then I remembered Doris telling me how her husband couldn't control his tongue, and it had gotten them into a lot of trouble during the Cultural Revolution. To avoid persecution, they had succeeded in fleeing to Guangzhou with the help of a powerful friend. I wondered if this mayor was that powerful friend because he didn't seem too concerned about the turn of conversation to topics that could result in a prison sentence. The mayor just made a few generic comments. But I stayed completely silent; I wanted to disappear through the floor.

Suddenly Doris' husband, looking sly, stood up and said he had to go to the market to buy some vegetables. About a minute after he left, Doris, furtively glancing from the mayor to me and back again, stood up and said, "I need to buy some meat at the market." Then she went out.

The mayor and I were left alone in the apartment! In my confusion, I suddenly realized what this was all about. I was supposed to give the mayor sexual favors so he would provide me with protection for doing my missionary work!

My heart was racing. I glanced at the door of the apartment. How fast could I run to the door if he made any advances? Would I make it in time? Had Doris locked the door from the outside when she left so I couldn't get out?

Lord, protect me from this man!

I watched the mayor's every micro-expression and micromovement for hints of aggression, but he seemed calm and relaxed. It seems he was waiting for me to make the first gesture of affection. I'm sure he saw how scared I was.

We carried on an inane conversation. I couldn't wait till my friends came back. Finally, after about *half an hour*, both Doris and her husband returned. They looked back and forth at us to see if their subterfuge had been successful.

After dinner just before I left, with a smug smile, Doris suggested the mayor and I exchange email addresses, and the mayor gave me a copy of the book he had written.

When I returned home our close Chinese friend, Peter, was visiting. I told him I had just met the former mayor and I showed him the book he had given me. "That's such a stupid book! It's all about how to get power. That mayor is full of himself." Peter made a face.

I told Justin that the former mayor had given me his email address and that Doris wanted the mayor to protect me if I got caught for doing our mission work.

Justin looked upset. "Don't email him! You've got to cut off this relationship. If the government ever catches us for our missionary work and you ask the mayor to intervene for us, you realize that you will have to teach English to his grandchildren, nieces, nephews, cousins, and anyone else he can think of! And it will take you all day every day to pay him back. Your life would be over. You would never have any time to do missionary work again. I'd rather we get caught by the police than use his protection."

Justin didn't yet know about the favor I had already been supposed to do for the mayor to pay for his protection. Only later did I tell him.

Fortunately, I never heard from the mayor again. I threw away his email address and his book. We continued sharing the gospel, trusting God for protection—God, who freely gives his protection without any quid pro quo.

THE SYNERGY OF GIFTING

Turn of the Century, Wuran and Huangdi

One Sunday evening, Justin and I were sitting in folding chairs in the downstairs of the Three-Self Church (the government church) in Huangdi. We were waiting to hear 60-year-old Mr. Niu teach the Bible for the very first time in this church of several thousand people. The astonishing thing was that until just over four weeks ago Mr. Niu had never even *read* the Bible! Justin had started teaching him the Bible only a month earlier, and then surprisingly, his church asked him to speak. We don't understand how it happened.

The few of us who knew that Justin was Mr. Niu's Bible teacher were not allowed to disclose that secret, even to other foreigners.

In church that Sunday evening, Justin and I were sitting by ourselves about 25 rows back and to the side, in the hope that it wouldn't be obvious we were friends with the speaker. But Mr. Niu shocked us—after he walked to the front to teach, first he faced Justin, then bowed a slow, deep bow to him from the waist! Justin and I panicked. We both slunk down in our seats, hoping no one would realize he was bowing to Justin. Of course, that probably just drew attention to us. Mr. Niu couldn't help but show his deep respect for

Justin, but we wished he hadn't done it so publicly!

Mr. Niu taught Genesis that evening because, as he later told Justin, "When the church asked me to teach the Bible, I didn't know anything but Genesis. I only knew that because that's what you taught me, so that was the only thing I could teach."

But Mr. Niu was a born teacher—years earlier he had taught high school. And as a Chinese, he was able to sinicize the whole teaching of Genesis, giving it an Eastern perspective and application.[18] I had to smile to myself—for this audience Mr. Niu was teaching the Bible far better than Justin could have ever done, even though his knowledge of the Bible was so limited.

We glanced around the auditorium while he taught. A lot of elderly people were furiously copying down every word he said. Later we found out they were house church leaders. Even though they were pastoring churches, they hadn't had any Bible training themselves, and they had probably never heard any teaching or preaching on the Old Testament because the government considered the Old Testament to be a threat to communist rule.[19] These pastors were copying down everything Mr. Niu said so they could teach their own churches the book of Genesis. After that first time, whenever Mr. Niu spoke, word went out through the house churches that he would be speaking and many, many house church leaders attended so they, too, could learn from his teaching and teach their churches.

As Mr. Niu's teaching time drew to a close that first Sunday night, Justin whispered to me, "We gotta get out of here fast! We don't want anyone connecting us to Mr. Niu, especially after he bowed to me."

---

[18] Aspects of Middle Eastern biblical culture are similar to Chinese culture, especially the family structure, certain issues of honor, the emphasis on the group over the individual, and storytelling.

[19] The Old Testament is a challenge to the Communist Party leaders' rule because the Old Testament makes clear that God is the one who rules over the governments of the world—raising up some and bringing down others. Also, the Old Testament contradicts evolutionary theory and the communist view of the progression of history through various stages, the final stage being communism. Since these concepts are fundamental to the foundation of communism, the communist government doesn't want the people of China to be exposed to the teaching of the Old Testament—the Old Testament is revolutionary!

But we were too late.

Before we had even walked to the end of our row, a man in his 30s rushed at us. He shoved his face into Justin's. "Who are you?" he demanded in Mandarin.

Before Justin had a chance to reply, he fired, "What's your occupation?"

Justin said, "I'm a manager." (Justin was a manager of a company at that time.)

"You're a teacher, aren't you?" the man sneered. He studied Justin's face.

"I'm a manager."

"You must be a teacher!" the man accused.

"I'm a manager."

"How do you know Mr. Niu? Are you his teacher?"

"I'm a manager."

Meanwhile we were pushing our way through the crowd as fast as we could, trying to shake the spy. We finally made it out the door and quickly flagged down a taxi. There was no time to wait for a bus.

Whew! That was a close call.

§§§

Just six weeks before Mr. Niu started teaching at the Three-Self Church,[20] when Justin was forming a new Bible school level class in

---

[20] The Three-Self Church was established in 1954 by the Chinese government. "Three-Self" stands for self-governing, self-supporting, and self-propagating. The church was created in order to remove foreign influence from the church and to make the church "patriotic" (euphemism for obedient to the communist government). In effect, it enabled the government to infiltrate and control the official Christian church. During the Cultural Revolution, Chairman Mao further tried to destroy the Christian faith by banning the Three-Self Church in 1966. Although it was difficult and dangerous, the Christians still worshipped, but secretly. When Deng Xiaoping became the leader of China, he realized that if the churches met secretly, then the communist government couldn't control them, so in 1979 he re-established the Three-Self Church in order to control Christianity. Some of these churches are good and are faithful to the Bible, and some are not. Many true believers worship in the Three-Self Churches, but some refuse. The house church members who wouldn't worship in the Three-Self Churches told us two reasons why they refused: they had watched the

Huangdi, *he had rejected Mr. Niu as a student because he wasn't qualified to even study in the class!* Justin's Mandarin-language class was designed for house church leaders who were mature in their faith and already doing ministry, not a man like Mr. Niu. How wrong we were! We didn't know how God planned to use Mr. Niu.

Justin had asked a well-connected Chinese evangelist friend of ours, Leon, to recruit house church leaders who would be interested in the training. He also needed him to find a safe location for the class to meet. After asking around, Leon found only one house church pastor besides himself who wanted the training. Justin was very disappointed because he had been hoping for a bigger class.

But Justin believed that God had put it on his heart to start this class, so he planned to go ahead with just two students.

Then Leon told him, "I've been looking for a safe location for us to meet, and I found just the place. The only problem is the place comes with a student, but that student isn't qualified to be in the class." Leon grimaced. "See, Mr. Niu is a manager, and we could use his office. I know he's not a house church leader or even in ministry, so he's not the kind of student you're looking for, but we can hardly meet in his office without inviting him. And actually if we use his office, him being there would solve the security problems—if he's there, it'll just look like we're doing business with him in his office and no one will guess that we're studying the Bible."

Justin and I discussed it at length. He didn't like the idea of lowering the bar so much. So he told Leon he didn't want Mr. Niu in the class, but Leon begged Justin to just meet Mr. Niu.

§§§

I had a very unusual role in Justin's ministry—a minor but vital contribution.

When we first married, Justin thought I was a gossip because after

---

Three-Self Church betray the house churches; and they said that the head of the Three-Self Church is an atheist government official, but the head of the true church is Jesus Christ.
https://en.wikipedia.org/wiki/Three-Self_Patriotic_Movement and personal knowledge.

we left a church gathering one evening I commented to him some things that no one had told me. "Barry's having an affair." "Leslie's a proud person." You can see why he thought I was a gossip.

He, and even I, for that matter, didn't realize I had been given the gift of knowing things about people that no one else knows. I don't entirely like this gift, but it does lead me to pray for what I see.

Justin's opinion of me changed one day after I told him exactly what someone's wife was like. We had never met her, but I knew her character because of how her husband treated me—and she turned out to be exactly what I had predicted.

I often feel like I'm a seeing person in a blind world.

My gift became very helpful in Mainland China when Justin needed to know the character of potential students for his Bible school level courses, especially whether or not they were spies. Justin often asked me to sit in on interviews with potential students for acceptance in the class. In each case, someone we were friends with had recommended the person, but we ourselves didn't know them.

I would sit to the side during the interview not saying a word, but noticing every raise of an eyebrow, every hesitancy, listening closely to unusual choices of words, which often indicated a desire to hide information. Afterward I would tell Justin, "Mr. Ma is a spy," or "Mrs. Xi is two-faced," or "Miss Li is trustworthy," ... Usually Justin hadn't picked up on any of it, but each time it turned out to be true.

When Mr. Niu came in, he was a little bald and he walked slightly hunched over. He wasn't at all what I was expecting—he didn't have the look of a proud, bossy, high-powered manager. Instead, he was serious and unassuming. He told Justin that he had been a Buddhist all his life until he trusted Jesus only five years earlier, but no one had ever taught him the Bible. In fact, he had never read the Bible and he didn't even understand much about the Christian faith. No one had discipled him at all. Mr. Niu told Justin that he knew he wasn't good enough to study in the class, but he still hoped Justin would accept him as a student.

Even though Justin wanted to teach people who had a more mature faith than Mr. Niu, I was gushing about him after he left. "He has such a beautiful spirit! He's so sincere and humble. He may not be the type of student you're wanting, but he is a prize."

Justin accepted Mr. Niu as a student and the four of them met in Mr. Niu's office.

§§§

In the first class Mr. Niu again told Justin that he wasn't worthy of being his student, so he would only audit the course. Justin told him firmly, "No one audits my classes. If you're going to be here, you're going to do the work!" He handed him a textbook.

The next time the class met, it became obvious that Mr. Niu was going to be one of the best students Justin had ever taught—he had spent each evening and the whole weekend studying the material, and he had an excellent grasp of the issues. He also asked many intelligent questions.

As impossible as it seemed, a few weeks after they began studying together, out of the blue, his local government mega-church asked him to teach on Sunday evenings. Then to preach Sunday mornings. Then to teach the adult Sunday school class. Then to train pastors on the outskirts of the city. It didn't make any sense because the government church only asked trained clergy to preach or teach.

Every time he preached, the place was packed with people standing in the aisles and crowded upstairs watching him on video.

Mr. Niu continued to teach whatever Justin had just taught him. When the class finished Exodus, Mr. Niu taught Exodus. Finished Leviticus, he taught Leviticus to the church …

After they finished Old Testament Survey, Justin taught the class New Testament Survey. After they started studying the New Testament, the church was treated to quality teaching on the New Testament.

And then Mr. Niu had the courage to teach about the Second Coming of Christ. That had never been taught in the government church since the 1949 Communist Revolution! It was strictly forbidden because it challenged the communist utopian ideals.

One Sunday evening, when Mr. Niu finished teaching, the congregation gave him *two* rounds of applause. You would have thought he would have been pleased, but he was very upset. He told

Justin, "Before I knew Christ I was a proud man. The Lord completely changed me and humbled me. But if they give me applause like that, I might become proud again. I'm so afraid that'll happen."

Then, suddenly, Mr. Niu's adult Sunday school class was canceled. After that he was told he was not allowed to preach Sunday mornings. Or Sunday evenings. Or train church leaders.

It wasn't because he had had the temerity to preach on Jesus' Second Coming, it was because the ordained pastors in the church had become jealous and they wanted this popular upstart out.

So the congregation protested. They wrote letters to the government authorities demanding that Mr. Niu be allowed to preach and teach. That is something you don't do in a communist country. But thanks be to God, after the protests and much prayer, the authorities relented and allowed him to start preaching and teaching again.

After they finished the New Testament Survey course, Justin wanted to teach the class basic theology using Charles Ryrie's textbook. It was time for them to grasp the theological issues of the faith. But we had no copies of that textbook in Chinese in China, and no one we knew in China had any copies.

Since the government censors often opened the mail, especially the international mail, we couldn't just order the books to be mailed into China; instead, we needed to find someone traveling to China who was willing to bring them in illegally and pray they wouldn't get caught. But first Justin needed to find three Chinese copies of the book, so he searched the internet for stores in the U.S., Hong Kong, and Taiwan to see if he could locate anywhere that sold Chinese copies of that text. But he couldn't find *any stores anywhere in the world* that sold *Basic Theology* by Ryrie in Chinese.

We prayed for this need. And we prayed. It was one of the many impossible things we had asked the Lord for.

Then Justin got a call from an old American friend of ours who had just traveled from the U.S. to our city in China. We hadn't known he was coming to visit. He told Justin, "I brought some books in. Would you like to come over and have a look?" He couldn't be more specific on the phone since calls were often monitored.

When Justin went to see this old friend, he opened his suitcase and there they were: the three Chinese copies of *Basic Theology* by Ryrie that we had prayed for!

If you're going to risk bringing random illegal books through customs into China, it wouldn't be these. The Lord had moved this old friend to buy the exact number of the exact textbook that the class needed. And to bring them to China—even though he didn't know if anyone needed them. And we still have no idea *where in the world* he had found them.

The men started studying again, learning the basic tenets of the faith.

It was God who had decided that he wanted Mr. Niu to be Justin's student, even though he wasn't qualified according to our thinking, and Mr. Niu went on to teach the Bible to thousands of pastors and laymen at a deeper level than they had ever had access to. These were people Justin would never have had the opportunity to teach. Each of us had played our part, using our God-given gifts to produce a work for the Lord together that was so much greater than any of our individual gifting alone could have produced.

And we learned that it is as important to teach one person as it is a thousand.

PARADOX

2000-2002, Wuran

Tense, I stood outside the door to Auntie's apartment, studying her. She stood on the inside, silently eyeing me.

It felt like a standoff.

Seeing what she looked like made me nervous. Auntie's large square face was topped with short-cropped hair. A little stylish. But it was her hard face and cold eyes that scared me. The only other Chinese women I knew who had cold eyes like hers were the ones with a violent past who had lived on the wrong side of the Cultural Revolution, bullying and murdering their fellow villagers. But I saw something else in her face that I hadn't seen in the others—a sweetness that shone through every now and then. I wasn't sure who she really was and I wanted to proceed with caution.

I was hoping to ask Auntie to disciple Rachael[21] for the year while our family would be in the States. Rachael was a university professor I had led to the Lord. It didn't feel good turning my friend over to a stranger, but I didn't know many mature local Christians,[22] and Auntie

---

[21] This was the Rachael from "Rachael and the Forced Abortion" in *Dragon Ride*.

[22] That's one of the difficulties of living in a communist country—it's hard to meet

came recommended. This visit was to help me decide whether or not to ask her.

After Auntie invited me in, she couldn't stop talking in Mandarin about the Lord—how she had become a Christian ten years earlier and how good the Lord had been to her. She also told me about the house church she attended. I relaxed and decided I would go ahead and ask her to disciple Rachael. She said she'd love to, that she had led another woman, Tina, to the Lord and she would disciple them together.

I breathed a sigh of relief. This was the answer to my prayers. After I introduced the two of them, I could leave for the States without worrying about Rachael. My heart sang as I left.

§§§

A year later, as soon as we returned to China, Rachael and I went out for a walk. Rachael was just a slip of a woman in her late 30s—petite, with a cute, small face, her hair cut in a short bob. Talking with her now, I could see how much clearer she was in her faith than when I had left. It made me glad that Auntie had discipled her; as a Chinese, she had done a much better job than I could have.

Then the two of us went over to Auntie's where I met Tina for the first time. She was in her early 50s; her thin face looked a little downtrodden, but I could tell she was a kind, honest woman, and I liked her.

Auntie, on the other hand, was mean to me in front of the other women, criticizing my clothes, my hair, and my Mandarin. I felt embarrassed and a little surprised. She hadn't been mean to me a year ago when I had met with her one-on-one. But in spite of her treatment of me, she finally turned to me and asked, "Grace, would you be willing to lead the weekly Bible study for Tina, Rachael, and me?"

Excitement coursed through my veins. This was a rare opportunity. The group was an extension of a house church, and this was the first time I had ever been asked by a house church to lead a study. I normally spent most of my time making friends with local people and introducing them to Christ, but I also loved leading

---

other local Christians. Most of the Christians I knew were people I had led to the Lord.

discussion Bible studies for women.

I wasn't sure why she was asking *me* to lead the study *she* had been leading. And after how coarsely she had just treated me, I felt guarded with her, so I told her to give me a few days to pray about it.

This study wasn't going to be easy to lead, but I wanted to do it, so a few days later I told Auntie yes.

What I didn't realize was that this was going to be a very significant group. Not only would the Lord use me to teach them how to study the Bible, but they were going to be facing some difficult trials that they would need my help to get through. I would also learn a lot—Auntie would teach me about prayer.

At the first meeting, the four of us crowded into Auntie's long, narrow kitchen to cook lunch. Before we started cooking, we talked in Mandarin about job and family concerns. Auntie was very caring; when I told her about a health problem I had, she immediately went to her medicine cabinet and handed me the Chinese remedy I needed.

But then, while we were cooking a popular local dish—noodles in a gravy-like sauce—Auntie chided me. "Grace, I can't believe you don't know how to make this sauce! Everyone knows how to make it." She laughed what didn't sound like a kind laugh. "Grace, what's wrong with you? You need to add more soy sauce!" "Grace, don't you know how long to boil the noodles?" And she burst out laughing again. I smiled a tight smile, but my face felt frozen in place.

After what seemed like hours, the cooking was finally over and I breathed a sigh of relief. We sat in Auntie's tiny dining area to eat some of the most delicious noodles I had ever eaten.

Then we prayed together. We didn't share prayer requests because over lunch we had already shared our deep concerns. After we bowed our heads to pray, I was alarmed—I heard someone crying! I couldn't figure out what was wrong so I slitted open one eye and tilted my head slightly. Auntie was weeping. "*Zhu, kelian women ba! Kelian women ba!*" ("Lord, have mercy on us! Have mercy on us!") She confessed her sins and prayed for our requests, crying the whole time. I was so moved! Never as a Christian had I sobbed before the Lord or brought my requests with such intensity. And what a humble way to pray—there was no room for pride.

After we prayed, I asked Auntie about it. She said, "Grace, we Chinese often weep when we pray. We need the Lord and his mercy so badly!"

Auntie completely changed my prayer life. She taught me how to approach the Lord emotionally naked. She showed me how to tap into my deepest feelings and weep passionately, pouring out my heart to God, asking for his mercy. No more "praying the way we're supposed to pray." Years later I realized that that was how Jesus prayed: "During the days of Jesus' life on earth, he offered up prayers and petitions with fervent cries and tears ..." (Hebrews 5:7).

But then, as I was tying my shoes and preparing to leave, I heard a malicious chuckle. "Grace, what a stupid way to tie your shoes!"

§§§

Later that week Tina and Rachael invited me to Tina's apartment for tea, just the three of us, no Auntie. Shortly after I arrived, it became clear why they had invited me when Tina said to me in Mandarin, "Auntie's a little mean, but you have no idea what she was like before she became a Christian. She was a Red Guard[23] during the Cultural Revolution, and she did some awful things to people as a Red Guard."

So the first time I saw Auntie I really had seen the face of a former torturer, possibly a murderer.

Tina continued, "I've known her for a long time and she was also my boss at the factory. Before she became a Christian, oh, was she ever horrible to me and the other workers under her. Although she's not very kind now, Jesus has changed her a lot. In fact, it was seeing the change in Auntie that convinced me to become a Christian."

Did I ever appreciate Tina telling me that this mean Auntie was actually a partially transformed Auntie! It took some of the sting away and gave me perspective.

§§§

[23] Red Guards were students who were part of a nationwide paramilitary movement, commissioned by Chairman Mao during the early days of the Cultural Revolution to further his political agenda. They were known for how violent and cruel they were.

At the next meeting, after cooking, eating, and praying together, we pulled out our Chinese Bibles to study the Gospel of John. Auntie opened her study Bible and announced, "This is the way we're going to study the Bible. We're going to read the passage, and then we'll read the notes at the bottom of the study Bible so we'll know what the Bible is saying."

"No, we won't," I countered. "We'll read the passage, then I'll ask questions so we can discuss the passage." If that's what Auntie wanted us to do, why was I even here? And what about all my hours of preparation to lead this study? But maybe she had never intended for me to lead the study at all.

Auntie retorted, "But we need to read the notes at the bottom or we won't understand it."

"No," I said firmly. "We'll understand it if we discuss it. This is the way we'll do it, through questions and discussion." If they themselves struggled to understand the Bible and apply it to their lives, I was sure it would be life-changing.

Auntie didn't know what to say—she had never studied the Bible that way. Also, I don't think anyone had ever stood up to her before because she was so mean. Furthermore, since I was only in my 40s, according to Chinese culture, I shouldn't have opposed her since she was my elder.

We read John 1 and discussed it using the questions I had prepared. Auntie was so surprised that we actually could understand the Bible and make it relevant to our lives.

§§§

One morning, when Rachael came to the study, fear was written all over her face. She told us, "My department head at the university told me this week that I have to become a Communist Party member or I'll lose my job!" She breathed in deeply. "But of course I can't become a Party member because I'm a Christian. I'd have to be an atheist in order to join the Party since that's the requirement. I don't know what to do—we need my income to survive!"

Auntie walked over. "I know the solution. There are eight other political parties in China.[24] You can use that to your advantage. You obviously can't belong to two parties. The Democratic Party doesn't require its members to be atheists. Quick join the Democratic Party, then tell your department head that you can't join the Communist Party because you're already a member of the Democratic Party."

Then Auntie looked Rachael in the eye and added, *"But I don't know why you don't just deny Jesus. All you need to do is tell them you don't believe in Jesus. That would be so much easier."*

I gasped. Lying is such a part of the Chinese culture, it's difficult for some Chinese Christians not to lie when the cost is high. Apparently, for Auntie that could extend even to the point of denying she believed in Jesus.

So I opened my Bible to Matthew 10:33 and read out loud the words of Jesus in Chinese, "But whoever disowns me before others, I will disown before my Father in heaven."

But before I could say anything more, Auntie snapped at me, "You don't know anything, Grace. *Peter denied Jesus. We're just following Peter's example. And Jesus forgave Peter, so we can deny Christ and afterward we'll ask his forgiveness. He'll forgive us, just like he did Peter. Then we don't have to give up so much. That's what I'd do if I were you, Rachael.*"

Since Auntie wasn't going to listen to me anyway, I let them hash it out. They argued back and forth. As the oldest, Auntie was supposed to have the final say, but maybe because we had been having a discussion Bible study where everyone's opinion was valued, Rachael was more courageous to oppose Auntie. It also became obvious how much Rachael loved the Lord.

Rachael finally spoke in an even, determined voice and clinched the argument against denying Jesus. "There's a big difference between Peter's denial and what you're advising, Auntie. Peter didn't *plan ahead of time* to deny Jesus. If the government forced you to betray your parents, like during the Cultural Revolution, in a moment of weakness you might do it. That's like what Peter did. That could be forgiven. But

---

[24] The other political parties existed in China to give the appearance of political openness.

how could you be forgiven if you *planned ahead of time* to betray your parents, even before the government tried to force you to? I will not deny Christ, even if it costs me my job!"

In the succeeding months Rachael held firm—she did not deny Jesus. She was able to join the Democratic Party and she wasn't fired.

§§§

Auntie seemed to have very conflicting emotions about me because I'm American. On the one hand she seemed proud that an American was leading her Bible study. I was a feather in her cap. But she also looked down on me because so much of what I did jarred her—I often didn't know how to do things the Chinese way. And she assumed that the Chinese way was the only way to act, so I was beyond the pale.

I also suspected that Auntie was trying to exert her authority over me with the other women. Putting me down in front of them was how to one-up me. For her it was a power play.

When I see power plays, I feel confused. They're hard for me to understand because I firmly believe everyone is equal since we're all made in the image of God.

Because of my strong belief in the equality of everyone, I have never found it difficult to treat Chinese people as my equals—neither superior nor inferior. Apparently, Rachael had seen my attitude clearly. One day when we went for a walk she told me, "I've only ever met one other American. He always looks down on us Chinese—he thinks he's better than us because he's American. But, Grace, you're not like that at all. You don't look down on us because we're Chinese. You treat us all as equals."

However, it's hard when you're treating someone as your equal, but they're determined to treat you as inferior.

§§§

Auntie's disdain finally got to me. The four of us went out to a restaurant one day. After enduring 45 minutes of being laughed at for everything I did—how I ordered food, how I ate, and what I said, I finally lost it. Standing up, I glared down at Auntie and yelled, "I've had enough of your laughing at me. Don't laugh at me again!"

"I don't laugh at you," she said defiantly.

"Yes, you do. Whether I eat, prepare food, or even tie my shoes, you laugh at me. It has to stop!"

Then I sat down, spent. I couldn't believe I had yelled at her publicly. That's even more gauche in China than in America because in China it's so important to give people face. Also, she was my elder.

But after that she hardly ever made fun of me again, and she even started to respect and value me. It seems that yelling at her had been effective.

§§§

Then one morning a few weeks after we ate at the restaurant, Auntie called a special meeting at her apartment. When I walked in, she was pacing, looking scared. I had never seen her afraid before. "As you know, Grace, we belong to a house church and Pastor Dave is our pastor. Yesterday he wrote us an email telling the time and location of our next house church meeting! How could he? We never communicate that information through email."

I shuddered, and as was my habit in China, my mind quickly assessed the damage. The Chinese government has access to all unencrypted emails, so the pastor had essentially told the government about their meeting, endangering all of them. And if these women were discovered by the police, because I was associated with them, even I and my other ministries might be in danger. Why was he being so stupid?

Auntie looked angry and confused. "I asked Pastor Dave why he did that since now the government knows about our house church meeting." Auntie paused. Then she spit out, "You know what he said? He said it doesn't matter because he has connections in America. He can immigrate to the U.S. anytime he wants, so he's safe. But what about us? We can't go to America. And he's our pastor! How can he throw us to the wolves and then run away?"

After a moment she looked intently at me. "We need you, Grace. We've been studying the Bible with you for almost three months. Could you help us understand why our pastor would do this to us?"

I had little to say right then; I was as confused as she was.

But in God's sovereignty, at the next meeting we were to study chapter 10 of John, about the Good Shepherd. As I prepared, I saw the passage in a way I had never seen it before—previously the hired hand hadn't seemed significant.

A few days later when we came together again, after many tears and prayers for the Lord's mercy and protection, we began studying. We started with a discussion about the basics of the passage. We talked about the Good Shepherd, Jesus—how he leads us sheep, protects us, loves us individually, even knows our names, and how he gave his life for us.

"So who are the thieves and robbers, and what are they like?" I asked.

"Those are the people who want to harm our faith and steal us away from the Lord, like Eastern Lightening,"[25] Tina answered.

After more discussion about the thieves, I asked, "And what about the hired hand? What's the difference between the thief and the hired hand?"

They struggled with this, so finally I said, "The thief comes to steal, kill, and destroy, but the hired shepherd, he isn't trying to harm the sheep. Instead, he watches over the sheep and takes care of them, that is, until it's too dangerous for him. He doesn't actually care about the sheep—for him it's all about the paycheck. He really only cares about himself."

"So when danger comes, he flees to America," Auntie added.

I nodded. "The Lord has given us little shepherds—pastors—to take care of us. They're supposed to be like Jesus, the Good Shepherd. But if they aren't willing to put themselves at risk to protect us like the Good Shepherd does, then they're just hired hands."

Auntie said, "We understand now. We know who Pastor Dave is."

I added, "But just because someone's a hired shepherd, that doesn't mean his teaching is false teaching. What a hired shepherd teaches may be good and helpful, but when there's danger, you better watch out. When the hired shepherd has to decide between his own welfare and that of the congregation, he'll choose his own safety every time. That's

---

[25] Eastern Lightening is a Chinese cult that kidnaps Christians to try to force them to convert.

when you know he was just a hired shepherd."

"That's exactly right," Auntie added. "He's not dangerous to you until there's danger."

The police didn't raid their house church, but Pastor Dave eventually did immigrate to America. That had been his goal all along. No one ever found out why he had been so careless and had put them all in danger with no concern for their safety.

The relationship between a missionary and the locals is often fraught with contradictions. Auntie had grown to respect me, but at a high price to me—I had had to endure a long road of disdain first.

And people can be paradoxical—quite a mixture of good and bad.

TOO STRONG A SENSE OF JUSTICE

2001, Wuran

One day Tina came to the meeting at Auntie's home looking a strange mixture of happy and sad. "My brother-in-law's body was finally released from the morgue! He had been in the morgue for nine years and my sister couldn't bury him. After all those years we can now bury him."

We were aghast and crowded around to hear the story.

"Nine years ago my brother-in-law was gambling with a group of guys at one of his friends' houses. The police burst in and stole the money! Although gambling is illegal, the police can't just pocket that money—that's even more illegal than gambling."

"So what happened?"

"My brother-in-law was so mad he went to the police station to tell the police they needed to give the money back." She turned to me. "In China you don't do that! You can't demand justice in China."

"Did they return it?" I asked.

"Well, the police told him they would get back to him. A few days later a policeman showed up at his workplace and asked him to come down to the station. He was all excited because he thought they were going to give him the money back." Tina's voice caught, "But we never saw him alive again." A tear slipped down her cheek. She quickly brushed it away.

Several of us gasped.

Now she sounded angry. "The police said he jumped out the window of the police station to kill himself. We know that didn't happen. The police killed him and threw his body out the window to make it look like he committed suicide. They murdered him!"

I knew that the police in China frequently tortured and killed prisoners with impunity, but her brother-in-law hadn't even been a prisoner when he was killed!

Tina sighed. "My sister also had too strong a sense of justice. She decided to sue the police!" Tina looked at me. "The judges do whatever the police want, so you won't get anywhere if you sue the police.

"The court case dragged on and on for nine years! You know why? The judge had to keep delaying so the real cause of death would never come out. And all that time the morgue was ordered not to release his body. Finally, my sister just gave up so she could bury her husband. It was a nine-year waiting game and they still won. They released his body from the morgue today. We're so glad we can bury him now. It's over."

"But what should your sister and brother-in-law have done?" I asked.

"They should never have tried to get the money back or tried to get justice. They should have just let it go. See what it cost them! In China you can't win against the police or get justice in the courts."

POLICE STATE

2000, Beijing

Nigel (16) and I were in Beijing for his doctor appointment when we decided to visit Tiananmen Square to play a game of "pick out the undercover cops." It's one of the things our family did for fun in a police state. Usually it was an innocent game.

Tiananmen Square is one of the sites in Beijing most visited by international tourists. The large, imposing, Soviet-style buildings of the central government surround the square, which covers over 100 acres. We stood close to the center of the square—on our right was Mao Zedong's massive, pillared mausoleum, and on our left was the Monument of the People's Heroes, the marble/granite obelisk as tall as a 12-story building. Almost everything in the square was communist-gray color.

"There's one!" Nigel said, tilting his head a little to show me without pointing, as that might have drawn suspicion. In a country like China, you don't want to draw suspicion.

"No, I don't think so. Look, he's meeting his girlfriend."

"How about that one?"

"I think you're right on there," I replied. "See his fine black leather jacket? I don't know how the undercover cops expect to be incognito when they all wear expensive black leather jackets. Also, look at his short, well-groomed hair, and his eyes, which are roaming all over the place studying everyone, even as he pretends he's just looking straight ahead."

"Yeah, he's one for sure," Nigel observed. "Look, he's talking but nobody's there. He's gotta be using comms."

Tiananmen Square was crawling with policemen that day. It seemed like every sixth person was an undercover cop.

Since the Chinese communist government doesn't want the appearance of a police state, throughout the country they use undercover cops liberally, but we were not expecting such a high concentration of them in Tiananmen Square that day.

On one end of Tiananmen Square, a red wall borders the Forbidden City, the ancient home of the Chinese emperors, separating it from the square. High up on this wall, a mural of Chairman Mao looks benevolently down on the people milling about the square. His portrait was not that calming, though, because all around us, every 40 feet on the square, we saw chandeliered lampposts covered with cameras pointing in every direction. The cameras were purposely not disguised, so their very presence tended to inhibit "anti-revolutionary activities." And maybe that was the reason for Chairman Mao watching us.

Near the edge of the square, white vans were parked about every 50 feet. Three large, darkened windows covered the side of each van, and two darkened windows covered the back. The vans had no markings on them whatsoever, but their purpose was obvious to anyone who has lived in China. These were the unmarked police vehicles for rounding up anti-revolutionaries.

About 50 feet from us, a woman in her 30s, standing in front of Mao's mausoleum, suddenly started tracing the outline of her body with her hands, from her thighs to her head. Nigel and I froze. We were pretty sure she was practicing Falun Gong exercises!

Before we could even catch our breath, six young men in black leather jackets surrounded her! We couldn't even see her anymore as they forced her toward one of the white vans.

A man pulled out a small camera to film the arrest. Other leather jackets rushed toward him and in the scuffle grabbed the camera away from him. The government wanted to make sure the world would not find out how they were treating Falun Gong practitioners.

After the woman was hauled away, several men sat down nearby on the gray granite tile ground and began practicing what looked like a strange form of yoga. Even more leather jackets surrounded them and dragged them into the waiting vans.

The Chinese government had been persecuting the adherents of Falun Gong, a cult derived from Buddhism, since at least 1996, when we moved to Mainland China, probably because they saw them as a threat. The Chinese communist government is insecure since it doesn't have the mandate of the people, so it sees a lot of beliefs and activities as threats.

Then in 1999 a group of about 10,000 Falun Gong practitioners traveled from Tianjin and surprised the government by staging a protest near the government buildings in Beijing. They were demanding that the government legally recognize their faith and stop persecuting them. How they succeeded in catching the Chinese government off guard like that is inconceivable. But the Chinese government doesn't like to be surprised, so after that demonstration, it set out to eradicate Falun Gong's at least 70 million adherents.

We only found out after we visited Tiananmen Square that day that in the months following the demonstration some Falun Gong protesters were dousing themselves in gasoline in Tiananmen Square and lighting themselves on fire in protest! We didn't know because the government controlled the media so tightly. I never would have brought Nigel to Tiananmen Square that day if I had known. In fact, I wouldn't have brought him if I had known he would be witnessing these arrests. It turns out police were rounding up Falun Gong protesters as fast as they could before they could immolate themselves. Fortunately, that didn't happen while we were there.

But as I also found out later, the "People's" Republic of China benefitted from arresting Falun Gong practitioners because they were harvesting the organs of some of them for transplant while they were still alive. Even their hearts and other essential organs were being harvested. Many of these organs were donated to Communist Party officials who needed organ transplants. (Some Christians who have been arrested have also suffered the same fate as some of the Falun Gong adherents, becoming unwilling organ donors, too.)[26]

Shortly after the men were arrested that day, at sunset, everyone crowded around the cordoned-off flagpole at the end of the square near Mao's portrait. We were all waiting for the ceremony of the lowering of the Chinese flag to begin. Four young soldiers in olive-green uniforms marched in formation toward the pole. With much pomp and circumstance, the yellow-starred red symbol of this great country was lowered.

In the crowd everyone was on edge. We felt a hush and everybody kept glancing around expectantly. Was a massive demonstration planned by Falun Gong, and might we get caught up in it against our will? Should we push through the crowd and get away before it started?

A couple of men in their 20s stood next to Nigel. One of them whispered to his companion in the *Cantonese* dialect, which is spoken in Hong Kong and the deep southern province of Guangdong, about 1,300 miles away. *"Baat dim jung wuih faat seng a."* ("It'll happen at eight o'clock.")

Quick as a flash, Nigel turned to them and asked in fluent Hong Kong Cantonese, *"Baat dim jung wuih faat seng mat yeh sih a?"* ("What's going to happen at eight o'clock?")

The men backed away with a look of shock and terror on their faces. They had thought that in Beijing they were safe telling their secret in Cantonese. But whatever the secret was, it was out now. How could they have guessed that an American teenager in Tiananmen Square in Beijing would be fluent in Cantonese and would overhear them?

We got out of there as soon as the flag-lowering ceremony was over, and I made sure we were on the bus leaving Beijing by eight.

We never found out what happened at eight o'clock because the news was so tightly controlled.

---

[26] *The Slaughter: Mass Killings, Organ Harvesting, and China's Secret Solution to Its Dissident Problem* by Ethan Gutmann (Amherst, New York: Prometheus Books, 2014).

THE AMBULANCE AND THE BEDPAN

2003, Wuran to Huangdi

The ambulance was idling, waiting for the Chinese head nurse to arrive so it could transport me from a private clinic in Wuran to the international hospital in Huangdi, 75 miles away.

I was frightened. For five days I had been very ill with a cyclical high fever that could last up to six hours, while I shook uncontrollably. Justin was away training house church leaders so I was alone. Finally, I had dragged myself to a taxi to go to the small international clinic in town. The doctor at the clinic had no idea what disease I had, so now I was lying in an ambulance for transport. But before the doctor was willing to put me on the ambulance, he spent five hours rehydrating me. Now that I was finally starting to urinate, I couldn't turn off the flow, so I told the head nurse that I needed a bedpan for the trip. But she had never heard of a bedpan.

As I waited in the ambulance, I looked around. The only equipment was the raised metal slab in the center I was lying on that acted as a gurney—no oxygen, no IVs, no medicines, no heart monitor, no cardiac defibrillator, not even a blood pressure cuff or thermometer—no medical supplies at all! Not even a sink! It was simply a transporting vehicle, not a means of saving a patient's life. But the important thing was, it looked like an ambulance from the outside—painted white with "ambulance" written in bold, red Chinese characters.

After 20 minutes, the head nurse popped her head in the door. She was a sweet woman in her early 30s with shoulder-length hair topped with a nurse's cap, and she was grinning from ear to ear. "I found one! This is what you were talking about, right? The thing you could urinate in during the ride?"

I nodded.

"So this is a bedpan!" She frowned as she stared at it from different angles. I noticed that the design of this bedpan was strange—the top and bottom were detachable from each other.

Then she told me, "I have no idea how to use this thing."

And she didn't. The first time I filled it, it came apart in her hands. Pee flowed down the aisle of the ambulance—there was so much it even formed waves whenever the driver braked or sped up! The nurse was very good-natured about it, but she didn't find it as funny as I did.

By the second time I used the bedpan, she had figured out how to keep it together. But there was nowhere to dump it since the ambulance was so basic. So, carrying the full bedpan while trying to hold it in one piece, she walked through the urine on the floor to the driver. Leaning into the cab section, she asked the driver to pull over to the side of the freeway. She jumped out and emptied the bedpan in the grass next to the speeding cars.

Even though it was only a 75-mile trip, it took the ambulance *four hours* to travel to the international hospital because the driver didn't know the way to one of the largest cities in China! All along the way he kept pulling over and asking directions! And once we entered Huangdi, he couldn't figure out how to locate the hospital. More pulling over and asking directions.

By God's grace, fortunately for me, my fever didn't spike during that trip, so I was able to enjoy the comedy.

I don't have a lot of memories of the week I spent in the infectious disease isolation ward of the hospital fighting for my life. After a few days a rash showed and I was diagnosed with measles. There was a measles epidemic in China that year. I was 49 years old at the time and I was told that 25 percent of adults who contract measles die. No one knows why my MMR vaccine didn't work.

But the Lord gave me the gift of humor and laughter in that ambulance with the bedpan before my battle with measles cranked up.

TRAINING RURAL HOUSE CHURCH LEADERS

Many years starting 2005, Mainland China

Code names in this story:
Maria (Grace)
Moses (Justin)
Tommy (police)

"Maria, I was seen!" I could hear the anxiety in Justin's voice.

Justin was calling from the walled-off site in the countryside, many hundreds of miles away, where he had been training house church leaders for two weeks. This was the last day of training.

"What happened, Moses?"

"I can't talk long," he said, his words coming quick. "I gotta get outta here fast! I was cleaning my shoes in the open area when a student unlocked the gate and let someone who wasn't part of the training come inside. Of course, no one's allowed to do that—it's too dangerous! The man might have seen me. There are no white people in this area, and if he reports to Tommy that he saw a white person here, it'll be bad for everybody. So the leaders decided to rush me to the airport right away before Tommy finds out I'm here. I'll call you as soon as we're outta here."

My heart was pounding. I knew the drill. If Justin were caught, the police would interrogate him non-stop for several days. Then he would likely be given 24 to 72 hours to leave the country. My mind was spinning.

The move would fall mostly on my shoulders. If we were kicked out, would any of the foreigners in our town be willing to help me move? Understandably, sometimes the other missionaries didn't want anything to do with a missionary the police had caught because they didn't want their own ministries to be implicated. I knew our Chinese friends would want to step up to help us, but we certainly didn't want to endanger them. The police would notice who was there for us and they might go after them.

So many thoughts and questions raced through my mind.

What would happen to our two cats? Who could we give them to at such short notice?

We had always tried not to keep much memorabilia in China just in case this happened, and now I was glad.

And when Justin called me from the training site, I myself was on a five-hour bus ride heading home from a doctor's appointment. I could hardly handle the anxiety. *Lord, please calm me down!*

Sitting on the bus, I waited for Justin to call back. And I waited. And waited. He said he would call as soon as he left the site, and I couldn't call him in case the police had already arrested him—all I could do was wait. And the longer I waited, the more sure I was that he was being interrogated, and that was why he wasn't calling me. *Lord, please help Justin handle the interrogation well and not betray anyone! And please help me. I don't know if I can manage such a fast move by myself, especially with my bad back.*

Finally, after *five hours,* Justin called. "Tommy didn't get me!" he said. "I'm coming home."

He hadn't called me sooner because his phone had been out of reach. He'd taken the SIM card and battery out of the phone and all three were in the back of the van so if the police did catch him, they hopefully wouldn't find the phone.

"It's five hours to the airport," he said, "and during the whole trip I couldn't get my phone because if I got out of the van someone might have seen me. We're finally at the airport now, so I was able to get it."

Justin hadn't felt safe even after they left the training site—they'd been on the run for five hours! If the police had arrested Justin and found his phone and SIM card, they would have discovered the treasure trove of phone numbers of our ministry partners. That would have been almost as bad as betraying them.

Chills ran down my spine, and I breathed a sigh of relief. The Lord had kept us safe. Again.

§§§

When Justin flew to a city to train rural house church leaders, the typical scenario went like this: Since the coordinator for the training had not met him before, he would ask Justin to wear a baseball cap when he got off the plane, so he could identify him. That made Justin laugh because he was the only white person on the plane.

When they met, Justin and the coordinator would exchange names. Not their real names. They would give each other a pseudonym, and that was usually the only name they would ever know each other by. The coordinator would lead Justin to a van with darkened windows and tell him to crouch down. Justin was then driven for hours to a location he didn't know. He wasn't told where he was going because they didn't want the police to ever be able to get that information out of him.

The van would stop in front of the stairwell of an apartment building, and the coordinator would jump out and run up the stairs to the apartment they would be using for the training to make sure the coast was clear. Only when the coordinator returned was Justin allowed to leave the van. As quickly as he could, Justin would race up the stairs to the apartment.

Once inside, he met the house church leaders who would be his students. Many were bi-vocational country folk who, in addition to being pastors, were also farmers or small business owners. Justin never knew the real names of any of the students, and they never knew his real name. That way if any of them, including Justin, were caught and interrogated, they couldn't disclose any names to the police, even under duress.

Inside the apartment, shades were pulled over the windows, the curtains were drawn, and the floor was covered with soundproofing. Often Justin wasn't allowed to leave during the weeks of training. In fact, he couldn't even peek at the sun during that time.

In some locations he wasn't allowed to keep his phone with him because the Chinese house church leaders were afraid the government would track it to the training site. During those times I prayed even more because I had no news from him. When he was able to keep his phone, he called every day, not just to talk with me and hear about our sons, but also to hear news of the outside world because he felt so isolated from everything outside the apartment.

§§§

There were times the house churches faced so much persecution the training was disrupted even before it started. Occasionally students couldn't show up because they had been arrested, or they were in hiding because their church leader had been arrested. One time at the last minute the location for the training was changed because the pastor of the church facility where Justin was to train was arrested for defending the rights of a village that was being forced out of their homes by the government, without even providing equitable compensation.

Since we lived in China Justin usually flew domestically within the country, but there were a few times when we were staying in America and he flew to the training from the U.S. One of those times was quite memorable. As soon as he landed in China, he turned on his local cell phone, and there was a text that said, "Don't buy your train ticket!" Justin didn't know what to do. Shortly after that his phone rang. "The training is canceled!" the man on the other end said. "The decision was made today by the local leaders as a precaution." Then the man hung up.

Apparently there had been a major security breach, but no details could be spelled out on the phone with the government eavesdropper listening in. Justin rebooked his flight back over the Pacific to America.

We were willing to live such tumultuous lives because the need for training house church leaders was so urgent. In some provinces there were so many people coming to Christ through the work of the house churches that in order to keep up with all the conversions, it was imperative that more pastors be trained as quickly as possible.[27]

Communism had tried to stomp out Christianity in China, but it hadn't succeeded. It was just as Jesus promised, the gates of hell could not prevail against the church (Matthew 16:18). The Chinese church had survived, but not without great suffering—many of the church leaders had been imprisoned, some for extended periods of time. And the Chinese Christians didn't have many Bibles. The house church leaders often told Justin stories about the times they didn't have access to Bibles, and how they had suffered for the Lord.

At the end of one teaching session, Pastor Li said, "The first time I ever saw a Bible was in the 1970s. And do you know where that Bible came from? *It had been dug out of a grave!* Before liberation [what the Chinese call the 1949 Communist Revolution] Christians were buried with their Bibles. It was a good thing, too, because after the Communists destroyed all the Bibles, we were still able to get ahold of some from the coffins of Christians. I was allowed to keep that Bible for seven days while I copied as much of it as I could. Then I had to give it up for another person to copy what they could for their use. The next time I saw a Bible was ten years later. I'll never forget the day I saw that second Bible—January 6, 1983. Oh, what a day!"

One young Bible woman (a female evangelist), Sister Zhang, told Justin one morning: "When I became a Christian in 1991, I was a kid and had almost no education, so I could hardly read. But I was good at copying Chinese characters, so I was one of the people chosen to hand-copy the Bible! I had no idea the meaning of what I was copying."

When they did have Bibles the Chinese Christians would memorize large portions of Scripture to prepare for times of persecution when they wouldn't have access to Bibles, or, like now,

[27] The government church runs their own seminaries to train their pastors. These seminaries were not open to training house church leaders.

when the communist government is significantly rewriting the Bible to paint Jesus in a bad light.[28] One time when I helped with the training, Sister Liu told me that when she was imprisoned all the Christian prisoners shared with each other the passages they had memorized. *They realized that among them they had memorized the whole Bible!* So in prison, through their memories, they had access to the whole of the Scriptures.

Brother Wang talked with Justin about "The Great Persecution," a severe localized persecution that began in 1997 and lasted for three years. He took Justin out to an old, small wooden building, and after entering he pointed to the space between the rafters and the roof. "That little space is where many of us Christian leaders hid for *three years!"* he said. "It didn't save us, though. After three years of hiding, we were caught and put in a hard labor camp."

Brother Hu told Justin at dinner one evening that in 1994 his house church network[29] sent 70 missionaries to spread the gospel to minority people groups throughout China. Those missionaries were called *Gan Si Dui,* the "Willing to Die Team," because they knew they might be killed for sharing about Jesus.

These precious Chinese brothers and sisters were sacrificing greatly to serve the Lord. Our sacrifice for the gospel was small.

At the time Justin was teaching the house church leaders, they did have access to Bibles—foreigners had been secretly carrying them in through the border for years. Later, Bibles were available for sale in the government churches, and during the five years between 2009 and 2013, they could even be bought *online* in China![30]

But the house church leaders didn't have any Bible study materials for training. They could only study from print books because most of the students were too poor to own a computer, and they weren't

---

[28] https://www.nationalreview.com/2020/10/chinas-communist-christ/

[29] The Chinese house churches have various "house church networks" that are associations of churches. A network was formed when a Christian brother or sister led many people to Christ (either in their hometown or by traveling to other towns or provinces). Those new believers led more people to Christ, which expanded that house church network.

[30] Personal knowledge.

computer literate anyway. Print books were a security problem—they were hard to print in country without being discovered, and to bring as many as we needed through the border illegally was very difficult. Through various means we did succeed at supplying them with study materials.

Even though Justin taught the courses in Mandarin, language was still a problem. In China, every province, city, and even many small towns have their own dialects. Many people who don't have much education in China can't speak standard Mandarin. They may understand it, but they communicate in their dialects. Usually the students could understand Justin's standard Mandarin, but sometimes he couldn't understand their dialects, so in these situations he needed a translator to translate their dialect into Mandarin so he could understand the discussions and their questions.

§§§

One time I accompanied Justin for a two-week training session in a walled-off site in the countryside. As our van pulled up to the gate, I couldn't wait to meet the pastors. Once inside the gate I looked around—the pastors were milling about the dirt "courtyard," which was surrounded by basic rectangular cement buildings. The pastors were short, thin country folk dressed in the unadorned, practical clothes of Chinese farmers, and they had a peacefulness and quietude about them. Many of them stared at me but seemed afraid to approach. They may have felt a little uneasy around a white person, but I suspect they were also afraid I couldn't speak Mandarin. And, of course, if they could only speak a dialect, I wouldn't be able to understand them anyway.

The almost 30 pastors who had come for training were of every age, from 16 to 80. There was no age limit to being a student. If someone was active in ministry, they were welcome.

About two-thirds of the pastors were women. Justin and his colleagues had encouraged more men to be trained, but they were mostly unsuccessful. In Mainland China, Christianity is thought of as a feminine religion, and the teaching about turning the other cheek only adds to that perception. So most of the believers in the churches are women, and it's very hard to find qualified male leadership. While the top leadership in these house church networks are male, most of the pastors are female.

The accommodations at the training site were spartan. The bed wasn't much more than a board with a thin blanket spread over it, and there was no heat, even in the dead of winter.

When I went to the bathroom, there was no sink or shower. The latrines were just troughs where the waste gradually migrated to a pit behind the "bathroom." I had seen worse toilets in China—at the training center all the intestinal worms were *inside* the toilet. I told Justin I could always tell what parasites the pastors had.

The house church leaders were used to less than sanitary conditions, but they knew the accommodations were hard on us, and they were grateful that we were willing to endure these conditions in order to train them. After a few days they gave us a large pitcher of water so we could at least wash our hands. I was so glad to have that water.

The first morning after we arrived, Justin and I slept in until six, but at five o'clock our Chinese brothers and sisters had already gathered in the classroom for prayer. When we walked in, they were weeping before the Lord, begging him for his help and mercy in their dire predicaments. The Chinese church is a praying church, and that's a major reason why it has been able to survive so much persecution.

I wasn't as gifted as Justin in teaching the house church leaders, so I eased his schedule by leading the morning devotions in Mandarin and teaching an optional basic English class in the late afternoons.

After a few days the pastors became more comfortable with me. Late one afternoon we were talking, laughing, and singing in the dirt courtyard when a leader who had organized the training stopped us. He looked at me kindly. "You are all having a lot of fun and you're quite loud. But if anyone outside these walls realizes that you, Grace, are a foreigner, the neighbors will report us." That put a damper on our comradery.

§§§

Training the pastors was very challenging for Justin—not just because of the spoken language issue, but because some of the students had only a second-grade education and they could barely read the Chinese study materials. Furthermore, most of them, regardless of their education level, didn't know how to analyze or think critically and they weren't comfortable with discussing alternate views. They always wanted to be told the "right answer."

But Justin was even able to make learning about the *structure* of a passage fun. In one session he turned a chair on its side and acted like he had never seen one before. "So, what do you use a chair for anyway?" he asked. "What's its function?"

"For sitting," they told him.

He then tried to sit on the side of the chair, then he tried to sit on the back of it. The students went wild. "No! No! This is how you sit on it!" One of the students demonstrated.

"Are all the parts essential?" Justin asked. "Some parts are just connectors, right? But if their sole purpose is to connect, are they important? Look at this screw here. I can hardly see it so it must not be important. I'll take it out."

"No, No!" they yelled. "The chair will fall apart without that screw!"

By the end of the object lesson the students realized that in a Scripture passage there are separate parts, connectors, and tiny hidden things, which are all part of the structure and serve the purpose of communicating the essentials of the passage. They were now excited to dive in to learn the structure of the passage they were studying.

When they studied Acts and Galatians, Justin drew a lot of heated debate from the questions he asked. "Was the early church in Jerusalem communist? How was it different?" "Why did the apostles hold the Jerusalem Council—was it because Peter or Paul was unclear about the gospel?" "Why was Paul asserting his independence from the other apostles?" Through all the questions and debates the pastors became more and more clear about what they believed.

In addition to the discussions about the passages of Scripture, Justin used skits to communicate the truths. Unexpectedly, the students added music, dance, and art to bring home the points of Scripture. Justin, who isn't very artistic, was so moved seeing them add their own cultural expressions to their understanding of the Bible.

In just a few days, I saw this group of pastors become creative, inquisitive, excited excavators of the truths of Scripture.

Justin taught Bible school level courses. There were a number of goals for the training, including teaching the pastors how to study the Bible on their own in order to strengthen their walk with the Lord, enhance their preaching so it would be more Bible-based, and equip them to defend the faith against all the cults that attack the Chinese Christian church. They were also encouraged to lead their own "second generation" groups so they themselves would be training up more leaders.

The teaching was successful. The top leaders told Justin that the pastors were no longer just using the Scriptures *as a point of departure* for their sermons. Instead, they were explaining and applying the Scripture texts in their sermons. And hundreds of second-generation groups were started. That meant that eventually the teaching could multiply without Justin—and that was the ultimate goal, to not be needed anymore.

KIDNAPPED!

2008-2012, Shi Liu

Justin and I had been living in the mega-city of Wuran for eleven years. But breathing the progressively gray air there was harming my respiratory system, so we decided to move to the small tropical town of Re Dai.

In this new area, we wanted to find a Three-Self Church to attend. The Three-Self Church was the government church of China, and we heard there was a good one in the adjacent town of Shi Liu, so one Sunday morning we biked the 45 minutes to that town.

As we rode along the one road that went through Shi Liu, we swerved to avoid a pothole. Then a small truck with its horn blasting drove us off the road entirely, almost into a parked motorcycle stacked with pomegranates. If we decided to make this our church home, getting to worship was going to be a life-threatening experience.

Shi Liu was a hub for selling pomegranates from all the surrounding pomegranate orchards. The fruit had ripened, and small trucks and motorcycles with flatbeds were loaded tall with pomegranates, on their way to or from market.

Because it was market day the traffic slowed to a halt as we entered the town, so we had to get off our bikes and walk them between vehicles. This was more than simply walking between parallel vehicles because the drivers had no sense of traffic lanes. The cars, trucks, and flatbed motorcycles were stopped at all different angles, crammed up next to each other, many almost touching. The traffic also spilled off the road, with trucks scooting around parked vehicles on the side of the road.

The town's buildings looked old. The walls were constructed of straw-colored, pounded earth, and granite-gray ceramic tiles formed upturned pagoda-style roofs. Still, I was shocked when locals told me the buildings dated back to the Song Dynasty—about 800 years ago! How had buildings made of earth lasted that long? Satellite dishes were secured to these ancient roofs, a mixing of millennia.

As we walked our bikes through the center of town, Justin spotted a cross on the left that stood taller than the buildings around it. We located the alley that led to the cross, and after walking past the walled dwellings lining the alley, we finally stood before the church. It was a very ordinary, unappealing structure, built of unpainted cement.

As we entered the 200-seat sanctuary, we saw that it was only half full. Most of the congregation were elderly women dressed in the rough clothes of farmers, probably pomegranate farmers. Only two younger women near the front were dressed in stylish outfits.

The sanctuary was plain-looking, except for a beautiful woven tapestry of Jesus as the Good Shepherd hanging on the right wall near the front.

The church was run by a family—a couple in their 30s, and the mother of the wife, Sister Ho. The sermon that morning was a solid message from the Word. This church preached the gospel, focused on Jesus, and even gave an invitation for people to come forward to give their lives to Christ. We decided that we were willing to bike the 45 minutes each Sunday and fight the traffic to make this our church home.

But no one greeted us. Not even one of the three pastors! Sunday after Sunday we came and went without so much as a Chinese "Good morning." We tried to reach out to the people, especially the pastors, but we hardly got anywhere. We wondered if they were uncomfortable with foreigners, or possibly there were spies in their midst and they were afraid to be friendly with us because of who might be watching.

In November, we were surprised when the church celebrated the American holiday of Thanksgiving. The church people loved that holiday because it was an extra excuse to give thanks to God. They didn't know anything about turkey or pumpkin pie; instead, they invited everyone to enjoy bowls of rice noodles in the vestibule to celebrate.

A few years after we started attending, Sister Ho, the older pastor, disappeared. No one said anything about her absence, and worship continued as usual.

Three weeks later she showed up again, and at the end of the service she walked up to the podium, and in a solemn voice said, "Three weeks ago I was kidnapped by Eastern Lightning. I was invited to a Christian meeting by a woman I had led to the Lord ten years ago, but it turns out it wasn't a Christian meeting she took me to but an Eastern Lightning meeting. The woman had converted to Eastern Lightning and she was kidnapping me! As soon as we walked in the door, people grabbed me! They forced me into a chair and tied me to it. Then they drugged my food and tried to brainwash me into believing that their Eastern Lightning teachings were true. They kept this up for a whole week."[31] Sister Ho looked very tense.

Eastern Lightning was a frightening cult. In order to make converts, they abducted and brainwashed Christians from house churches, usually pastors and young Christians; young Christians because they assumed they wouldn't be solid in the faith yet, and pastors because they were the most influential. But this was the first time I had ever heard of Eastern Lightning kidnapping anyone from a *government church*. Once a Christian was abducted, if he or she converted, the cult would send them back to their church to lure even more Christians to their meetings in order to kidnap and convert them. If the Christian didn't convert to Eastern Lightning, the cult would usually mutilate or murder them, or they might threaten their family. There was a saying among the Chinese pastors, "Hand me over to the

---

[31] For a more detailed account of a Chinese pastor who was kidnapped by Eastern Lightning, see *Kidnapped by a Cult: A Pastor's Stand Against a Murderous Sect* by Shen Xiaoming and Eugene Bach (New Kensington, PA: Whitaker House, 2017).

police any day, but please, whatever you do, don't ever hand me over to Eastern Lightning!"

Sister Ho continued, "I finally tricked them into thinking that I believed their teachings and had converted to Eastern Lightning. That's why they let me go."

I stifled a gasp. If she hadn't converted, how did she convince them that she believed the Eastern Lightning teachings? And especially without denying Christ? But what bothered me even more was that I suspected she actually had converted to Eastern Lightning—that was the obvious explanation for why she had been released. I was horrified. How was I supposed to deal with my own pastor having been kidnapped by a cult, likely having converted, and now possibly trying to lure me, too? This was more than I could take.

We knew another Chinese pastor, a house church leader, who had also been captured by Eastern Lightning. Afterward, everyone, including the other Chinese pastors, was afraid of him. Justin and I didn't know if he had converted to Eastern Lightning and would help the cult snatch us away, too, so we were also careful around him. Even as foreigners we weren't safe—we knew of a German man who had been kidnapped and had converted!

Sister Ho went on, "They threatened me that if I ever told anyone they had kidnapped me, they would *kan tou* (chop off my head)." Her hand slashed her throat to make the point.

But here she was, telling us publicly about the kidnapping! I had no idea what to think, and I was scared.

Then she told us what Eastern Lightning believed—that Jesus has already returned to earth as a *Chinese woman*. And she explained biblically what was wrong with their beliefs—that when Jesus comes again it will be a major celestial event, and we shouldn't believe anyone who says that Jesus has already returned to earth until we see him in the sky (Matthew 24:23-31).

This was encouraging. Maybe she hadn't converted after all, but I was still very apprehensive.

After that she warned us, "Don't trust *anyone* in the church! They might be part of Eastern Lightning and want to kidnap you!" How's that for good fellowship?

When the service was over, our heads were spinning.

As we biked home, I asked Justin, "Do you think our pastor has converted to Eastern Lightning?"

"No. She wouldn't have told us all that happened if she had."

"But Eastern Lightning doesn't free people unless they convert. And if they don't convert, they kill or mutilate them—she even told us that they would kill her if she told!"

"But she told us what's wrong with their beliefs, so she can't be Eastern Lightning."

"Couldn't that just be a trick? I don't know what to do. This is our pastor. How can I trust her if she asks me to her home or to go to a conference? She could be planning to kidnap me!"

We kept attending the church, and as time went on I could see that Sister Ho was solid in the Lord, and I became convinced that she had not converted to Eastern Lightning.

Then one Sunday as I sat in church, I looked up at the woven tapestry of Jesus as the Good Shepherd, and it struck me. As our pastor, Sister Ho was just like Jesus, the Good Shepherd, who had been willing to give up his life in order to save us. She had risked her life to tell us what happened to her and to warn us about Eastern Lightning so we would be safe.

By God's grace, at least during the rest of the time we lived in Re Dai, Eastern Lightning didn't kill Sister Ho.

STEPPING UP AND BACKING AWAY

2009-2012, Re Dai

In Re Dai, Justin worked in the administration at a government university, and one of his responsibilities was to interview students for jobs. Out of the blue at the end of one interview, the student, whose name was Eve, asked him, "Do the foreigners in this city have a Christian fellowship?"

Justin was immediately on guard. That's the type of probing question a spy would ask. When we wondered if someone was a spy, we usually didn't give any information; instead, we asked questions to assess if the person was for real, so Justin asked her why she wanted to know.

She said, "I just returned from a three-week group trip to America. It was sponsored by an American school and was designed to give us cross-cultural exposure. My host family were Christians, and was I ever impressed with them! They loved on us so much. It was the first time I had ever met a Christian, and I'm so attracted to the Christian faith because of them. So I want to find a foreign Christian fellowship to attend."

It sounded genuine. Spies usually only want to *find out*

information, they never *give* any information.

Justin was so excited. He couldn't invite her to the foreigners' fellowship because the government would quickly shut it down if any local Chinese attended. Instead, he asked me to talk with her and see if she had come to believe yet, and if not, to lead her to Christ.

A couple of days later I invited her to our home. Most Chinese women are very feminine, but Eve looked almost masculine, with her strong, stocky body and short, no-nonsense haircut. We spent some time conversing in Chinese to get to know each other. I liked her—she was straightforward, intelligent, and curious.

Then I asked her who Jesus is and how a person becomes a Christian, but she had no idea. All it took was a few simple explanations and she joyfully embraced Christ. It had been a cooperative effort, each part of which had been essential. Her host family had created a desire in her for the Lord through their love and by talking with her about Jesus, Justin had introduced her to me, and I led her to Christ.

Eve was the first student in Re Dai that I introduced to Jesus, and did she ever commit herself to him! She began reading the Bible a lot and sharing her faith with her friends. She came over to our home often, and I loved watching her faith grow.

It was essential for Eve to get to know Chinese believers, so we brought her over to talk with Amy, a 50-year-old Christian professor at the university. They already knew each other because Amy was the one who had led the trip to the U.S., but Amy's faith hadn't made any impression on Eve whatsoever, even though they'd spent three solid weeks together.

The thing is, Amy was a secret Christian. She was afraid of her faith becoming public knowledge because there was so much at stake—she might lose her position as a professor.

For almost the whole trip, even when they were in America, Amy kept her faith a secret. Then finally, only just before the group returned to China, Amy felt convicted that she needed to tell the students she was a Christian, so with trepidation she announced to them that she was a follower of Jesus. But at that point it was really too late, and neither her faith nor her confession impressed the students. If she had naturally talked about Jesus all along instead of just making an announcement at the end, the students might have been more attracted to the Lord. Even so, *that was a turning point for Amy.* At last, she had openly admitted to being a Christian.

The second turning point for Amy came when we told her that Eve had become a Christian. After that, Amy decided that she really did need to be more open about her faith, regardless of the risk.

The next turning point came when we told Amy that Eve wanted to be baptized. She surprised us by stepping up to the plate. "I want to baptize her myself." Step by step, Amy was coming out of the safe bubble she had created for herself.

It's quite hard to find a secure location to baptize a new believer in China, but Amy knew just the place. She rented a hotel room *for an hour* to baptize Eve in the bathtub! We gathered with a few other Christian college students we had introduced Eve to.

The joke just before the baptism was: "What do you think the hotel staff thinks we're doing here—in this room rented by the hour?"

"Well, they certainly won't guess we're performing a sacred rite—and one that's illegal!"

We watched as Eve came up out of the water. She was glowing with her new life in Christ!

But Eve was struggling in ways I wasn't aware of. One day she called me. "Grace, I need to talk to you right away. I'm really upset about something."

When she came over, she told me, "My father is a high-level policeman in Zao Gao City [the largest city in our province]. You realize that he is in charge of making sure people don't become Christians? Well, he is really angry that I, his daughter, became a Christian. He's also angry because before I committed my life to Jesus, I was applying to become a Communist Party member, but now I'm planning to withdraw my application. I would have to be an atheist to be a Party member, but I'm not an atheist anymore."

"So what will this mean for you and your family?" I asked.

"Well, that's the problem—my grandpa is so upset he's riding the bus down here *right now!* He's coming to try to talk me out of following Jesus. He feels that strongly." She sighed. "I'm real close to my grandpa. And as you know, that five-hour bus trip is a pretty rough ride, and it's extra hard on him because he's in his 70s." Her breath caught. "I so wish he weren't riding that bus on account of me."

I reached out and touched her shoulder. She was shaking slightly.

"How are you feeling about the fact that he wants to talk you out of believing in Jesus?"

"I'm really, really scared. As you know, I need to obey my elders."

"So what are you going to do?"

She looked up at me. "I've decided to deny that I believe in Jesus. It would just be words—it won't be from my heart, so it won't matter. But that would make my grandpa feel better. I really don't want him to be so upset."

"Eve, when we believe in Jesus we can't deny him, even if we're only saying words that don't come from the heart." I showed her what Jesus said in Matthew 10:32-33. "Whoever acknowledges me before others, I will also acknowledge before my Father in heaven. But whoever disowns me before others, I will disown before my Father in heaven."

She jarred up. "Then I can't deny my faith in Jesus, no matter what it costs me." She looked distressed, then she looked off into the distance and thought for a few minutes.

With determination in her voice, she said, "This is what I'm going to do. Before my grandpa can say anything, I'm going to set the ground rules. I'll tell him, 'My faith in Jesus is non-negotiable. Now let's talk!'"

She went into the confrontation with her grandpa strong and came through even stronger.

But the conflict with her grandpa was only the beginning of the serious battles Eve would face for her faith. When summer came, she went home to stay with her family, but it seems that her faith suffered from facing so much daily pressure from them over such an extended period of time without having anyone to strengthen her in the Lord.

When she returned after the summer break I was so excited to see her, but every time I called she wouldn't pick up the phone or call me back. I texted her, but she didn't reply.

So I asked Amy if she had gotten in touch with Eve. "No, she won't answer or return my calls."

I asked the Christian college students Eve knew, but they couldn't get any response from her either.

One day I bumped into Eve on campus. All excited I said, "It's great to see you, Eve!"

She looked away.

"We should get together," I continued.

"I don't have time." She looked nervous.

"Just for a few minutes?"

"No, I'm busy."

I walked away, confused and sad.

We finally did hear through one of the Christian students that she was still following the Lord, but she wasn't ready to be in contact with any of us believers.

What had happened? Years later I wondered if her father was using his high position in the police department to monitor all her calls and listen in on her face-to-face conversations through her phone. That would explain why she was afraid to even speak to me. But at the time I didn't think of this and it just felt like personal rejection, especially since she wouldn't tell me the reason.

Now that it was crystal clear that she didn't want to see me or talk with me, I dropped it and didn't try to contact her again, but I was really hurt. When you pour yourself into someone, then they turn their back on you, it's painful.

But I didn't realize that I hadn't forgiven her or that I even needed to forgive her until the next time I saw her *three years later*. We were about to move from Re Dai when I was strolling down the "walking street" on campus. A walking street is a street barred to vehicles and crammed full of vendors and food stalls. There Eve was, sitting at a table with her friends, talking and laughing.

When she saw me, she jumped up, ran over and hugged me!

I stiffened.

Then she asked me, "Could we get together? I'd love to see you, and I really want to talk with you."

I stood there mute, staring at her, thinking about how much she'd hurt me.

I walked away.

How could I have walked away from her? That was ten years ago and I never saw her again. What had she wanted to tell me?

Lord, please forgive me for holding resentment in my heart until it was too late. And please send someone better than me to help Eve on her faith journey.

SOME THINGS ARE WORTH THE RISK

The Students of the Mandarin-Language Bible Study at Re Dai University
Introduction
2009-2012, Re Dai

Rex, an Australian missionary, looked shaken when I bumped into him on the street. "The police set up a filming crew across the street from my home with a telephoto lens aimed at my apartment," he said. "And they are filming *everything going on inside my home!*"

The police had already terminated Rex's contract as a professor at Re Dai University [32] for holding large English-language Christian meetings for students in his home. And now this. How far would the police go?

So Rex stopped the meetings, and eventually he and his family just packed up and left Re Dai.

But in the time he had been able to minister to students, Rex had made quite an impact for the Lord. Although it's true *anywhere*, it's more obvious in China—you have to grab opportunities to serve the Lord for as long as you have them because opportunities don't last

[32] The police were effectively in charge of the universities, and they could terminate professor contracts or kick a student out of school.

forever (Ephesians 5:16).

§§§

It was in this environment that the Lord put a desire in Justin's and my heart to start a small Mandarin-language Bible study for Christian college students. We hoped that if it was small, it wouldn't be noticed by the police. We knew it was risky, but some risks are worth taking. And by God's grace we were able to avoid detection for almost three years.

However, our initial difficulty wasn't the police; it was that we knew almost no Christian students. For a year we prayed that the Lord would open the door for us to start a Bible study. When God finally did make it happen, it was fast. One day at a tea house we met a Christian woman who wasn't associated with the university, and yet within a few days she had introduced us to Mark, "the most influential Christian student on campus." Within a few weeks Mark had gathered other students for the Bible study and we were able to start. But it turned out that on this campus of 10,000, Mark was only able to find ten Christian students for the study.

Mark was tall, thin, and friendly. A Hani minority student, he had become a Christian in his village before attending college. He was suffering for his faith at the university as the police kept interrogating and investigating him for actively sharing Christ on campus. Although Mark was fully aware of the danger he was in, he always looked happy and easygoing, never worried about the persecution. His life belonged to Jesus, and he trusted the Lord with the outcome. And he was undaunted; the police didn't succeed at intimidating him, he continued to serve God all through the interrogations.

On the evening of the first Bible study, Justin and I biked the 45 minutes to our campus apartment[33] and set up snacks. This apartment was on the second floor of a small apartment building. As time for the study approached, we heard laughter and loud footsteps coming up the stairs. I cringed. If it was the students, I wished they'd be more quiet—

[33] We had two apartments—the city apartment we lived in and the campus apartment provided by the university as partial compensation for Justin's work there.

we didn't want to draw attention to them gathering at our apartment.

The footsteps *were* the students, eight of them. And as they filed in, I glanced at the security motion detector the university had installed on the *inside* wall of the apartment. Had the police put it there so they could see and hear us through hidden cameras and bugs? This was the first time we had done any group ministry in the apartment. But since the police didn't barge in on our meeting, we came to the conclusion that the motion detector didn't actually work. It had been installed just to intimidate us so we wouldn't do any ministry there. *Thank you, Lord.*

Over the three years we ran the study, a variety of ethnicities attended: in addition to Han Chinese, we had many minorities—Yi, Bai, Dai, Hani, Naxi, Lisu, Pumi, and Manchu. Most of these minority groups were the native inhabitants of this part of China before the Han Chinese conquered it. Every minority people has its own culture, customs, celebrations, traditional dress, and language, and most of them don't look like Han Chinese.

When these students invited us to their homes, we saw the poverty of their families and villages, often surviving by subsistence farming. During a visit with one Lisu student, her parents were so grateful for the spiritual input we'd had in their daughter's life that they treated us like royalty, giving us the best seats and cooking a delicious Lisu dinner for us. But their amenities were very basic. They had no electricity, no indoor plumbing, and there were almost no walls surrounding the living area leaving it open to the elements, even during the cold winter months. When I needed to go to the bathroom, I was instructed to go into the middle of the cornfield and do my business there! Fortunately, it wasn't yet harvest time so I had some privacy.

Most people in these minority villages had little education; many hadn't studied past third grade. In one village, I was shocked to see 14-year-old girls who were already married with one or two kids in tow! The girls in their early 20s had aged prematurely and already looked like old women. The parents of the students we knew had saved their children from such a fate, and often at great financial cost to themselves had made sure their kids were educated right through high school and now in college.

During the time we lived in Re Dai, the government was trying to encourage minority teenagers who showed academic promise to get a college education, and many of the minority students in our Bible study were the first people in their villages to go to college.

One female Hani student told us, "My whole village is putting their hope in me getting a college education. In fact, after I was accepted to college, in order to make sure I would be able to go, the entire village pooled their resources to pay for my tuition and expenses because my family didn't have any money." It only cost a few hundred U.S. dollars a year.

Since the people in China are very communal in their thinking, the village's hope was that this one student would climb the ladder of success and reach down and pull the rest of them up. That was a lot of hope and expectation resting on these minority students' young shoulders, and it put in perspective for us the risk they were taking to attend our Bible study. If they were caught, it might jeopardize the hope of their entire village.

THE BEST PARTY IN TOWN!

The Students of the Mandarin-Language Bible Study at Re Dai University
Part 1
2009-2012, Re Dai

The Lisu, one of the minorities represented in the Bible study group, look quite different from the Han Chinese—their skin is darker and more brown-toned, their eyes more rounded, and many have oval faces. But what really set them apart was that a lot of them professed to be Christians. About 100 years ago, James Fraser, a missionary from Britain, led many of the Lisu to Christ. Because so many Lisu claim to be Christians, the Chinese government actually considers Christianity to be the religion of the Lisu, and the police don't tend to come down so hard on them for their Christian faith.

In the beginning the faith of the Lisu people was vibrant, but now, several generations later, although 90% of the people in these Lisu villages still profess to be Christians, many of this younger generation know little to nothing about the Bible or their faith. The faith has not been passed down well to the succeeding generations.

A few weeks after we started the study, four male Lisu students started attending. They were the great-great-grandsons of the people

James Fraser had led to the Lord, but even though they regularly attended church in their Lisu villages, none of them had ever even heard John 3:16 or Psalm 23!

When we asked them, "What is a Christian?" they scrunched up their eyebrows in confusion and asked, "*Someone who lives a moral life?*" That was the best they could come up with.

Since they didn't seem to know much about the Lord, Justin asked them why the people in their village go to church. They laughed and said, "*It's the best party in town!*"

Justin and I debated how to get these young Lisu men excited about the faith. We were studying Galatians and Romans with the group, but we needed something more. Then new believers who started to attend put the beauty of the Christian faith on display for them. One of these new believers was Leila.

One day Justin and I, along with a group of seven students, were discussing how much the Lord has changed our lives since we became Christians. Leila, a vivacious Han Chinese girl with thick, shoulder-length hair spoke up. "My foreign English teacher led me to the Lord a few weeks ago, and I am so grateful! I was a nasty person before I came to know the Lord, and I hated everybody. But now, because I follow Jesus, I *have to* love everyone—I have no choice. It's really hard, and I feel like I'm suffering for Christ when I love people.

"You would think that would turn me off to believing in Jesus," she said, "but I wouldn't want it any other way—I'm so glad Jesus is changing me because I hated who I was before knowing the Lord."

Leila paused and, with resolve in her voice, concluded, "And if the police figure out I've become a Christian, there is nothing they could do to me that would make me give up Jesus and go back to the way I used to live before knowing him."

I looked around at the students. They were deeply moved by Leila's powerful testimony, just as I was. The students who had already been turned on to Jesus because of our study now pursued the Lord even more as a result of hearing how the Lord had transformed Leila and the other new believers.

We hoped that what Leila said would also stimulate the faith of the Lisu, and they did look excited, but it didn't last. Neither the testimony of the young believers nor our studying Scripture was enough for them. We were only able to give them what they were willing to receive. Maybe all they wanted was "the best party in town."

HOW COULD GOD DIE?

The Students of the Mandarin-Language Bible Study at Re Dai University
Part 2
2009-2012, Re Dai

Joyce was a petite Han Chinese girl with a fiery personality. One of the students invited her to the study because her foreign teacher had told her about God and she wanted to find out more. Everything we studied in the Bible elicited a passionate question from Joyce. One evening she was so irritated she started shifting around in her chair. She spit out, "Why did Jesus have to die? Couldn't God just pardon everyone without Jesus dying? There was no need for that sacrifice." After attempting to answer her question, the Christian students finally came up with the answer that God is not just loving, he's just. And justice means there has to be punishment for wrongdoing.

"Then how could Jesus die for my sins when I wasn't even born?" She almost sounded like she was taunting the faith. The students debated that question, but couldn't come up with a satisfactory answer, so finally Justin entered the fray. "Because Jesus is the Son of God, his sacrifice is sufficient to cover everyone's sins no matter when they were born." Justin opened his Bible. "Turn to Hebrews 7:27: 'He sacrificed for their sins once for all when he offered himself.' This was once for all time, so his one sacrifice is good enough for all eternity, and that includes you, Joyce."

Then she asked indignantly, "Why did God send his *Son* to die for us instead of dying for us *himself*? Now, if God had died for us *himself* instead of just making his *Son* die for us, now that really would have shown how much God loved us." One of the students smiled, "Because Jesus is God." Joyce gasped. Then the students tried to explain the Trinity.

Finally, after she understood what they were saying, she looked appalled. "But how could *God* die?"

Every question she asked had a profound effect on the believing students. Often her questions made them realize how confused they were about their faith, and as they struggled to find answers, they began to take what they believed more seriously and understand their faith more clearly.

After weeks of having her questions answered by the group, Joyce told them, "I get it now. I want to become a Christian." She went back to her foreign Christian teacher, who led her to Christ and baptized her in a bathtub, with her friends as witnesses.

§§§

Leo was a Han Chinese friend of Joyce's who also attended the study; his mother was a Christian and he professed faith in Christ, too. He was tall, thin, and a little effeminate, and he was very affectionate with me. He, too, was a curious person, like Joyce.

After Joyce was baptized, Leo asked if I would be willing to meet with the two of them once a week in addition to the regular study because they had so many questions about the Lord and the Bible that couldn't be answered in the group setting.

The first time we met, Leo brought 13 pages of single-spaced typed questions for me to answer! They were all good questions. In the first session, we succeeded in discussing only one inch of his questions! We laughed a lot, and they had many aha moments. But I did notice that Joyce was more subdued when Leo was around. I couldn't understand her change of personality.

After a few months, things went south with Joyce and Leo. They didn't act like they were involved with each other, but from things Leo said it seemed like they were taking the Lord's commands about sexual conduct lightly. I wasn't sure where Joyce stood—I couldn't get much response out of her anymore.

One day Leo asked, "Is it OK for Joyce to warm up the homeless in her bed?" I was confused. When I referred to the homeless women that Joyce was "warming," Leo corrected me. "Joyce is sharing her bed with homeless *men* on cold nights in order to 'warm them up.'" Leo said it with a smirk, and I felt like I was being toyed with. Really, Joyce was having sex with homeless men? I tried to talk more with them about sexual purity, but Leo couldn't understand why it would be a problem.

And furthermore, why was Leo telling me these things about Joyce that would be so personal and maybe embarrassing to her? What hold did he have over her?

When Joyce was about to graduate, I asked her what job she was going to get. Instead of Joyce answering, Leo said with big grin, "Joyce is planning to be a porn star!" My eyes widened. I looked questioningly at Joyce, but she didn't respond.

No matter what I said, Leo was confused by the idea that following Christ meant they needed to obey the Lord, including living sexually pure lives.

Answering their 13 pages of questions had been useless. Faith without obedience is not the faith the Bible talks about (Romans 1:5; 16:26).

I really wanted to meet with Joyce one-on-one because it was obvious that meeting with the two of them together had been a mistake, and Leo was pulling Joyce away from her commitment to the Lord. But I couldn't meet with only Joyce because Leo insisted on the two of them coming together, and Joyce wouldn't stand up to him.

I hardly got together with them again after that—it had just become a game for Leo to shock me.

Later some believing students in the study told me that Leo was a bad person. I've learned that when Chinese people are willing to tell me that, I need to listen. But it was already too late.

When June came, Joyce graduated and left the area without even saying goodbye.

A few months after that, Justin and I were laying low because students from the Bible study were being interrogated by the police to try to get information out of them about our study.

Leo was a year behind Joyce, so he was still on campus. One day he called and said he urgently needed to meet with me. I agreed, but I insisted that we travel separately to a restaurant in the city, away from campus, where each table had its own separate room cordoned off by a curtain. But the curtain didn't reach the ceiling, and just outside the curtain was the kitchen and central waitering area. I didn't think it'd be a problem because we could talk quietly.

But then, toward the end of the dinner, Leo became angry and told me how an authority at the university had mistreated him. He started yelling in Mandarin, "I'm going to kill him! I'm going to kill him!"

Here I was, a foreign woman in my 50s, out eating lunch with a male college student while trying to keep my activities hidden from the police, and the student is yelling for all to hear that he's going to kill a school administrator! I kept looking around, expecting to be dragged off. Nothing happened and I left as soon as I could. But I never met with Leo again, and that was the last time I ever showed my face at that restaurant.

THE DANCER

The Students of the Mandarin-Language Bible Study at Re Dai University
Part 3
2009-2015, Re Dai

"I don't want to go back home to my village after I graduate." Brave looked at me with fear in her eyes. "My uncle might kill me!"

"What are you talking about? Why would your uncle kill you?"

"He's a warlock. Whenever someone offends him, he casts powerful spells on them. He's killed many people in my village using his spells. Most of my extended family are dead because of him! I don't want to go back there."

I gasped. She was serious.

We'd merely been discussing what she was going to do after graduating from college, but this was the reaction she had, thinking about moving back to her family's village. I didn't know what to say. I hadn't known there really were people in Mainland China who practiced such dark black magic.

Brave was one of the most solid members of our student Bible study. She never, ever wanted to miss.

Her face was so expressive—she often looked at me with the pureness of joy, or with the raised eyebrows and openness of a question mark written on her features, or a sadness that crept through even when she tried to mask it. The flowing way she draped a scarf over her head and shoulders or how she tilted her figure made it obvious she was artistic. Although Brave didn't have the slender, floating body I associated with dancers, she was a professional singer and dancer, and her performances were beautiful, graceful, and emotive. Whenever she was around, she expressed such richness of feeling that being with her was a feast for the soul.

Brave was of the Hani minority, and that may have been where her music and dancing talents came from since the Hani are famous for their singing and dancing.

Even though the Hani, as a people group, are polytheists, Brave's family had converted from polytheism to believe in Jesus. After that, the government tried to persecute the Christianity out of them. In spite of all the police interrogations and threats, Brave, as well as her mother, brother, and sisters held firm to their faith, but as a result of the persecution, her father turned against the Lord. Not only did he turn his back on Jesus, but *he* began to persecute the family as well. The rest of the family continued to stay true to the faith, even with this second onslaught of persecution coming from one of their own. Brave's father was a controlling, violent man, but Brave was careful how she talked about him. When she did, though, a stiffness and caution swept through her body.

§§§

Brave was so excited about the Lord. When she entered the university, she told Justin and me that she was determined to lead all the students to Christ. That actually was her goal—but what a risky goal! It would have quickly made her a target of the police.

I guess she thought that once she left her village, she had left the persecution zone.

We tried to slow her down a little and explain how things work in a university in a communist country—that she certainly could and should share about Jesus, but it had to be done discreetly and cautiously, or she might be kicked out of college. But what we said sounded like nonsense to her. It's very hard for a Chinese person to believe that we foreigners know anything about *their country*.

Six weeks later, when she talked to us again about sharing her faith, she didn't even try to hide her depression. But the problem she was facing wasn't even the one we had warned her of. "No one wants to hear about Jesus," she said. "When I talk about him, my roommates just laugh or ignore me. I'm not going to be able to lead anyone to Christ." She hung her head.

A wise Chinese Christian friend of ours named Roman was visiting from Wuran that week, so Justin told him about Brave and introduced the two of them. Roman was an evangelist in Wuran so he understood how difficult sharing the gospel in this communist country was. Justin was hoping that Roman, as a Chinese, could say something to Brave that she would trust, since she wouldn't believe us foreigners.

The next time we saw Brave, she was glowing. "Roman said that most people don't want to hear the gospel, so I have to live out the gospel first in order to earn the right to speak. He told me that I should serve my roommates in any way I can, like sweeping the floor of the dorm room. After they see me living so much like Christ, they may be open to listening to what I have to say about the Lord."

Eventually, she was able to share Christ with her roommates.

§§§

Justin talked with the students about forming their own student-led fellowship in addition to our Bible study. Brave took up the challenge. There was no place for them to meet, though. If they met in the dorm, they would almost definitely be reported. The only place they thought might be safe to gather was outside after dark! So this group of Christian students met outside at night, come rain or moonlight.

§§§

One afternoon when Brave visited me, she showed me her legs—whole sections were inflamed, blistery red. "I've had this disease for a long time, and it's really painful."

I prayed for her healing, but the Lord didn't heal her. I didn't realize that the Lord didn't want to heal her through my prayer because he planned to bring healing to her spirit.

I suggested Brave see the doctor, but she didn't even have the few dollars it would cost, so I took her and paid for the visit myself. Whatever the skin disease was, the doctor couldn't diagnose it or cure it—I guess the consultation was only worth a few dollars. But my taking her to the doctor bound Brave's heart to mine; after that, she told Justin and me that we were her second parents because we loved her so much and took care of her needs. And I could see a transformation come over her—after that she looked calmer and more secure, like she felt more safe because of our strengthened relationship.

§§§

A few years after she graduated, Brave and her boyfriend, Tim, wanted to get married. But her father wouldn't approve of their marriage because Tim was in Christian ministry and not making a lot of money. Since, according to Hani culture, she had to have parental permission to marry, she asked Justin and me to take on the role of her parents to decide if she could marry Tim.

So, on the day Justin and I were finally moving back to the States, Brave and Tim traveled hundreds of miles to the airport so we could meet him and give our approval. We liked Tim a lot—he was a sweet, engaging, young man who loved the Lord.

A year later, Justin flew halfway around the world to attend their wedding. As a couple, Brave and Tim are now risking themselves daily for the sake of the gospel.

And because Tim wasn't from her parents' village, Brave didn't need to move back there and risk being murdered by her uncle.

THE POLICE KNOW WE'RE CHRISTIANS BY OUR JOY!

The Students of the Mandarin-Language Bible Study at Re Dai University
Part 4
2009-2012, Re Dai

Harry, a Han Chinese student, began attending our Bible study after his foreign English teacher led him to the Lord. Harry was a shy, nervous student, but through knowing the Lord he blossomed and became more outgoing. He had only attended the study for a month, when without warning, he disappeared. People disappearing in China is not a good thing.

Six weeks after he disappeared, he was again knocking on our door a few minutes late for the study. We couldn't stop hugging him and laughing.

After several minutes of animated conversation, the group settled down. Harry sat in a white easy chair. "I have something I need to tell all of you." He paused for a moment and his face looked pained. "The police have been interrogating me relentlessly for the past six weeks. It's been really hard. I haven't been coming here so they wouldn't discover the group." He sighed. "They've been interrogating me because I became a Christian."

"How did the police know you had become a Christian?" someone in the group asked.

"My teacher makes everyone in our class take a psychological assessment questionnaire once a month to find out if any of us have become Christians," Harry answered.

One of the other students commented quietly, "We all have to fill out those questionnaires."

This assessment was an attempt to look inside the students' brains to see their thoughts and emotions. Is nothing safe in a Marxist country?[34]

Harry continued, "See, before I started following Christ, I was really depressed, and I wanted to kill myself. Whoever evaluated that questionnaire knew that from the results. But now that I know Jesus, I'm not depressed anymore—I want to live and I'm so full of joy. They picked that up on my assessment six weeks ago and figured out that I'd become a Christian! That's why the police started interrogating me—they're trying to force me to give up my faith in Jesus."

"Wow!" one student exclaimed. "So they would rather you be depressed and suicidal than full of the joy of the Lord?"

And the police can tell who's a Christian by our joy? Why don't *they* all become Christians then?

After that Harry told us, "The police taunted me with a lot of arguments against Christianity that I had trouble answering because I'm just young in the faith. But I've held up under the interrogations."

When he left, we thought the reason he had come to the meeting was because the interrogations were over and it was safe to rejoin the group again. But apparently he had made a calculated risk to attend the Bible study only once to tell us about the interrogations and to warn us. He was hoping the police wouldn't catch us if he came only once. We knew that we shouldn't contact him because the police would know—

---

[34] A Marxist state isn't just concerned with controlling how its citizens act, but also how they think, because Marxism is on the totalitarian spectrum. Hence, the indoctrination of children in school and the propaganda that masquerades as news. Maintaining a free thought-life based on truth is critical to living free in a Marxist nation, but it's also dangerous.

we just had to wait for him to contact us.

We never saw or heard from him again.

ALL MY EDUCATION HAS BEEN IN VAIN!

The Students of the Mandarin-Language Bible Study at Re Dai University
Part 5
2009-2015, Re Dai

Normally we gathered in the living room of our one-bedroom campus apartment. The main door of our living/dining area opened right onto the hallway of the apartment building, so it was a little unsafe, but since we were at the end of the hallway and we had never had an unscheduled visitor, we didn't worry about it too much.

Then one evening, because the Chinese FBI was trying to locate the Christian group they had heard about on campus, we decided to meet in the *bedroom*, because there would be an extra door between our Bible study and the hallway. Anyone who came to the main door wouldn't so easily discover the students, and hopefully the sound of our discussion wouldn't travel into the hallway.

A dozen students, mostly men, came that night. We had set up a few chairs in the small space beside the bed but most of the male students sat sprawled on the king-sized bed.

That evening, well after all the students had arrived, someone did knock on the door! Our first unexpected visitor! Justin and I glanced at each other, uneasy. Then we signaled for the students to be silent. Justin quietly closed the bedroom door before opening the main door of the apartment to see who was there. The visitor, whatever his real motive in knocking on our door was, never saw or heard the dozen students crammed in the bedroom.

Two students whom I already knew, Fabian and Horatio, had been invited to the meeting that night. Although both were still atheists, they were curious about Christianity. Fabian and Horatio were quite different from each other—Fabian was thin and intellectual; Horatio was strong and fun-loving. Horatio usually looked absentminded with a slight smile playing on his face, like he was thinking about the last prank he had played.

Before we began studying, Fabian looked over at me puzzled. "Grace, before we start, I have a question I want to ask you. This is something I've been thinking about a lot. Does your hair really grow out of your head already curly? I can't figure out how that could happen!" None of the students laughed because this was a serious question. Before knowing me, they had never met anyone with naturally curly hair, so it was something many of them had been wondering about.

After I unsuccessfully answered how curly hair could actually grow out of my scalp, we opened our Bibles. Fabian and Horatio didn't say much during the study.

Toward the end of the Bible study, Fabian spoke up. "Everything we studied here assumes the existence of God, but how can I know if God exists? That's what I'd like to understand."

The face of one of the students sitting on the bed lit up when he heard the question. His name was Blaze and he was a very sweet guy who loved the Lord. His parents were Christians and he had been well-versed in apologetics by his father, but he wasn't such a deep thinker. All excited, Blaze told Fabian, "When Jesus rose from the dead, his disciples saw him alive, so did the women who were following him, and then *500 people* saw the risen Lord! There's our evidence right there."

I cringed. Since I had been an atheist once myself, I suspected that his "proof" wasn't going to mean much to these atheists. Fabian and Horatio didn't want to humiliate Blaze, so they sat there silent.

I hated breaking with my fellow Christian and I didn't want to embarrass him, but I knew that if I didn't speak up Fabian and Horatio would assume this was our best evidence and they would think it was something to be dismissed. I had to wade in.

I turned to Blaze. "I appreciate your evidence and your knowledge about the subject, Blaze, but when I was an atheist what you just said wouldn't have convinced me." Blaze looked at me shocked. Fabian and Horatio stared at me wide-eyed and breathed a sigh of relief.

I continued, "The reason why it wouldn't have convinced me is because you have to trust the biblical accounts when they say that all those people saw the risen Christ. If you're not sure the Bible is true, then why would you believe it when it says something like that?" Fabian and Horatio were looking at me with avid interest. I wasn't going to accept a "proof" that wasn't convincing just because I wanted them to become Christians.

Horatio asked me, "Then why do *you* believe in God, Grace? What would convince a person?"

I stayed on the subject of the resurrection. There was so much I could say, but I wanted to keep it short since not everyone in the group had this question. I only baited them. "We know from non-Christian sources outside the Bible that the Romans crucified Jesus at the Jews' insistence. After they crucified him, neither the Romans nor the Jews wanted anyone to claim that Jesus rose from the dead as he had predicted he would do. That would have been worse than never having crucified him. So why didn't they produce Jesus' body to stop the rumor that he rose from the grave?"

Both Fabian and Horatio were nodding and thinking deeply. But neither came to Christ that evening.

A few days later Fabian texted me. "I need to see you this afternoon, Grace. Can I come over?"

After he sat down on the couch, he told me that he was having a real hard time believing in God. God didn't create the world—everything just came from the Big Bang.

Because I had thought a lot about this from leading other students to Christ, I had a diagram of the Big Bang ready in the coffee table drawer. I took it out and showed it to him. "Do you know why scientists postulated the Big Bang?" I asked.

He looked very interested in the question, but he shook his head. He moved forward to sit on the edge of the couch.

I said, "They discovered that the universe is continuously expanding. If it's expanding, then it must have had a beginning."

He nodded thoughtfully.

I continued, "There was no material universe before the Big Bang. That means that everything that is physical came from a source that is not physical."

He gasped.

"And that is exactly what the Bible says." I showed him Hebrews 11:3 "… what is seen was not made out of what was visible."

Then he made a comment that shocked me. "*All my education has been in vain!*" He looked disheartened. "My teachers taught me about the Big Bang, but they never told us what the implications were. You've given me a lot to think about, and now I'm leaning toward believing the Bible.

"But I have one last question. My Christian girlfriend told me that when Jesus comes again, we will be raised from the dead. That's way too hard to believe! How can our bodies be raised from the dead? Worms eat us and we become soil. This is stopping me from becoming a Christian."

I had never been asked this question before by an unbeliever. But by God's grace I had recently read I Corinthians 15 in my devotions, so the answer was on the tip of my tongue. "When you sow a seed of wheat, do you sow the wheat plant that comes up?"

He looked at me with curiosity but didn't say anything.

I continued. "The seed you sow has a different body than the plant that sprouts, but you can see how the one comes from the other. It's the same with our bodies. There's a correspondence between our present bodies and our resurrected bodies, but they're not identical, just like the wheat seed and the wheat." (See 1 Corinthians 15:35-37.)

He sighed, sat back on the couch and relaxed. "That answers it. Thanks."

He still wasn't quite ready to become a Christian. In fact, right after graduation he broke up with his Christian girlfriend, whom he was very much in love with, because his mother told him he had to. According to his mother, Christians don't make much money, so he wasn't allowed to marry one.

But that wasn't the end. He couldn't stop thinking about Jesus and a couple years after graduation, against his mother's wishes, Fabian committed his life to the Lord.

NO ONE LOVES US LIKE YOU DO

The Students of the Mandarin-Language Bible Study at Re Dai University
Part 6
2009-2015, Re Dai

Faith[35] was a petite Han student who dressed a little classier than most of the other students. Whenever she looked at me, her face broke into a gentle smile that exuded intelligence.

She had known the Lord since childhood, and her parents were missionaries to a remote part of China. I felt a sense of awe being around her because I could tell she had a close walk with the Lord; and it wasn't just *I* who ministered to *her* spiritually, she also ministered to me. One day, after I told her about a problem in my family that deeply grieved me, she invited me out to McDonald's to tell me about a similar situation in her family that the Lord had completely turned around. "I told you this, Grace, to encourage you that the Lord can make the impossible happen in your family, too." Oh, did I ever appreciate this student.

Three years after our Bible study started, our group was discovered

[35] This is Faith from "To Betray or Not to Betray" in *Dragon Ride*.

by the Chinese FBI when the agency interrogated a Christian student whom they scared into betraying us. After that, they went after Faith, who was the student we used as the point person. We had thought it was safer for us to contact only one student with arrangements for the study and have her relay the information to everyone else. That probably saved us for a while, but eventually, since the FBI has access to all phone records, including recordings of calls,[36] it put Faith in the hot seat. They realized she was the point person and the one they needed to interrogate in order to get more actionable information about Justin and me.

Although Faith was a strong person, the interrogations were very hard on her because she was trying so desperately to protect us. I ached for her when she told us what she was going through for our sake and the gospel's. She never did betray us, and it turned out that all those difficult FBI interrogations made her even stronger in her faith and commitment to the Lord. She learned to be fearless—she had faced the giant and survived. A few years later, she started on a journey of serving the Lord and sharing the gospel in bold ways that could land her a long prison term.

Since the FBI was coming after us, we decided we needed to move out of the area, so in a secret location we trained both Faith and Brave[37] to take over the leadership of the Bible study. The study was finally going to be completely student-led, and that only happened because we had to leave.

But there would be no safe place for the group to meet after we left because our apartment would no longer be available. Meeting outside after dark wasn't going to work for a Bible study. Then it struck me: there was one dorm room where I had led *all* of the women who lived there to the Lord, so their room was a safe room. That was where Faith and Brave moved the Bible study to.

As the time was nearing for our departure, we begged Faith and Brave not to go to the bus station to send us off. We were afraid

---

[36] We were told by a foreigner who was interrogated by the police that during his own interrogation they played back recordings of his phone calls to incriminate him.

[37] This is Brave from "The Dancer," and from the story "To Betray or Not to Betray" in *Dragon Ride*.

plainclothes policemen would show up at the station to watch who came, and we didn't want to further endanger them. But they wouldn't be deterred; they came anyway. They couldn't help but show their love for us, no matter what the risk.

§§§

Two years later, when we were well settled into our new home in Kao Shan, Faith called me. She was so upset she didn't even bother to speak cryptically on the phone. She was breathing rapidly. "Grace, I've got a big problem and I need your advice," she said in Mandarin. "Before, it was the *An Quan Ju* [Chinese FBI] who were interrogating me. After you left they stopped interrogating me, but now it's the *jing cha* [local police] who have started interrogating me.

"But my real problem is that when Ranger [a house church pastor we both knew] was being interrogated, he gave the police my phone number! He strongly advised me to call the police. That's when the police started interrogating me." Her voice broke. "Ranger betrayed me! I can't believe it—I trusted him."

Whose side was Ranger on? Justin and I were friends with Ranger. I didn't think he always made the best decisions about security, but I knew he loved the Lord and the Lord's people. He would not purposely betray Faith. The police in China are very devious and evil. I suspect they were threatening Ranger to get him to convince Faith to call them.

I decided to defend Ranger; I hoped I was making the right decision. "Think about it, Faith, when the police were interrogating Ranger, he was probably given no choice but to divulge *some* information about you. Since the police already knew your phone number, he didn't tell them anything they didn't already know. He may have actually protected you by *only* giving them your phone number, and it may have been the best he could do to protect you."

I could hear her breathing slowing down. "OK, that would explain it. Then I can still fellowship with Ranger."

It seems the police tactic in this situation was to drive a wedge between the Christian leaders by giving the impression that one had betrayed the other! It would break their fellowship and unity.

§§§

Half a year later in our new town a rumor reached our ears that Ranger had converted to Eastern Lightening. I didn't believe the rumor because of how well I knew Ranger, but just in case, it was important to investigate it because he was influential with a lot of the students in Re Dai whom we had led to the Lord and discipled. Even at a distance, we still had a role in shepherding them. So I traveled 11 hours on buses to visit the students and Ranger. After talking with Ranger for an afternoon I could tell he was still the same godly Ranger I had known, and that the rumor had no basis whatsoever—it turned out the rumor had been started by someone who had an agenda.

Then I went out to eat with the students to encourage them in the Lord. As soon as Faith saw me, her eyes welled up with tears as she spoke for the group. "Grace, since you left we haven't found anyone to love us like you and Justin did!"

When I returned home, I told Justin what Faith had said. He laughed, "As important as our teaching of the Scriptures was, what moved them most wasn't our 'great' Bible teaching, it was our love for them."

SURROUNDED

2006, The Bering Sea

"Mom, one of the Somali guys died this morning!" Adam's voice was streaked with sadness. After graduating from high school, Adam had moved back to America. He was calling me in China ship-to-shore from the large fishing boat he was working on, which was docked in a harbor on Saint Paul Island in the Bering Sea. This was one of the fishing boats run by a major fishing company that provides America with her frozen fish.

I was aghast. "How did that happen?"

"We were processing crab. Apparently, a certain percentage of people are allergic to crab and get what they call 'crab asthma,' but they don't know they're allergic to it 'til they're around crab. The Somali came down with it.

"The island of the harbor we're in has only about 400 residents. It has a clinic, but the clinic didn't open 'til 9 a.m. He was dead by 7."

"Why didn't they call the doctor to come in early?"

"They don't have his number."

"But they often dock in that harbor. It just makes sense that they would have been proactive and kept his phone number on file, especially since a certain percentage of the workers do come down with crab asthma." My voice was breaking. The needless disregard for this man's life.

"And why didn't they stock EpiPens® and Benadryl®?" I asked. I knew the answer. Because they didn't care about human life.

"His cousin also works on the boat," Adam said.

"He must be grieved."

"He didn't have much reaction. He's Muslim, so all he said was 'Inshallah,' it's Allah's will."

§§§

Why was my son employed on a dangerous fishing boat in the Bering Sea?

Adam, like all of us, had difficulty adjusting to America because Eastern culture is so different from Western culture. Adam spoke two Chinese dialects, and in China some of his closest friends had been Chinese, so Chinese ways of thinking, speaking, and behaving were natural to him. American ways felt so foreign.

We had come back to the States for half a year to help him adjust, but it wasn't enough. We would have given up our ministry in China and moved back to America to be there for him, but we didn't realize soon enough how hard it was going to be on him. And Justin and I didn't understand American culture very well anymore either, so we weren't much help to him, even in just finding a job or housing.

When he moved to the States, Adam had an affinity for internationals—he often lived with Sudanese refugees or other Africans. But then between jobs, when he couldn't find a place to live, he took the job on the fishing boat in the Bering Sea.

If we had been in the States to offer him temporary housing while he looked for a job, he might have found a better job and not have worked on the boats.

§§§

The Bering Sea was full of beauty and wonder for Adam when he was able to leave the confines of the lower deck of the ship where he worked.

Saint Paul Island is one of four volcanic Alaskan islands located in the middle of the Bering Sea. When Adam walked across the island, it was just a solid patch of ice. Snow and hail fell constantly, stinging his skin in the high winds. About a hundred compact houses huddled together on the island. They looked assaulted in the harsh conditions. The majority of them were owned by Alaskan Natives, or Aleuts, most of whom worked in the fishing industry. There wasn't much to the town, but it was striking that there was an onion-domed Russian Orthodox Church. It seemed that the Aleuts on Saint Paul Island prioritized their faith.

The island was surrounded by icebergs floating in the sea. While docked at Saint Paul Island, though, the captain wasn't careful so their ship completely froze in the ice. It took several weeks to dig a channel to release the ship.

Adam was astonished when he disembarked on another island—bald eagles had landed everywhere. This dot of an island in the Bering Sea was the only resting place for the bald eagles on their migration north.

But Adam could enjoy the beauty only on rare occasions. Mostly he was stuck on the lower deck with 70 other workers doing the back-breaking work of processing fish. They were given few breaks, and the breaks were brief—15 minutes to eat and maybe eight hours of sleep.

The fishing boat was the job of choice for ex-cons and some immigrants, mostly men, who also couldn't find a better job.

The workers slept two triple bunks to a room. On one of Adam's earlier calls to me, he was distraught. "Mom, four guys in my room put porn up all over the walls. I don't have the right to take it down and I don't know what to do. Please pray for me!"

And did I ever pray!

On the next call, Adam was excited. "Mom, you'll never believe how the Lord answered our prayers. About ten percent of the workers were sent back to the Mainland for misbehavior or injuries, but in my room two-thirds were sent back—exactly those four guys who had put up the porn! The Lord did this for me. After they left, I took down all the porn." But that was nothing next to what Adam was about to face.

Adam was open about his faith on the fishing boat, and the men didn't treat him well as a result.

One day when he called from the ship, he seemed subdued. "Mom, I had a narrow escape." He paused. "Since many of the men are ex-cons, they're quite evil. Every day they talk about drugging my food and raping me. Normally we work 16 to 24 hours at a stretch, and that keeps me safe because they have no free time. But then we docked in Dutch Harbor and wouldn't have any work for 72 hours. All the men were real excited talking about all the fun they were going to have drugging me and raping me."

I could barely breathe hearing this.

"But the Lord saved me! The thing is, they all got drunk the night before they planned to do it, so early in the morning I crept out of the room while they were hung over and still asleep. I disembarked on the island. I figured I had to go somewhere they wouldn't look for me, so I went to the library. They'd never look for me in a library! Those three days were great—I spent the whole time reading. I only slipped back on board to sleep when I knew they would all be drinking in the bar. They never found me, and in fact, since I was missing, the captain even sent out a search party to find me!

Thank you, Lord!

We had begged Adam not to work on the fishing boat, but it was his decision. All I could do was pray, and the Lord heard our cries.

One day in his weekly phone call Adam told me about one of his shipmates. "There's this guy, Greg. He grew up in a Christian home, but he turned his back on the faith. Well, Greg told me that his whole mission in life is to destroy the faith of anyone who believes in Jesus. There aren't any other Christians on the boat, so of course he targets me. But how he goes about it is laughable. He tries to get me to say curse words. What's so tempting about that? It's just stupid!"

He sighed. "I was so tired of all these people that when the foreman asked who would like to work in the freezer I volunteered. It's usually an alone job."

Working in the freezer in the Bering Sea? And that's his job of choice to get away from his coworkers?

Adam added, "It's an extra-dangerous place to work because they don't lash down the pallets of frozen fish. If the boat lurches while you're next to a stack of pallets, they could fall on you and kill you.

"One day Greg also volunteered to work in the freezer with me. That kind of defeated my purpose. But it turns out he wanted to talk to me alone. He told me that he has succeeded in turning a lot of people away from the Christian faith, but before meeting me he had never met anyone who was the real thing—one who loves the Lord like I do and isn't a hypocrite."

Such mixed feelings welled up in me. Adam's light for the Lord was shining clear and bright. But the danger he was in! The Lord would need to keep protecting him.

Adam later told me, "When you admit to being a Christian in a non-Christian environment, you're being watched all the time because they want to see if you will fall. They end up respecting you if you don't, but you never fit in. The worst thing is to let them know you're a Christian and then give in and live a compromised life—they are all gleeful that you are a hypocrite and, although they will welcome you into their group, they will despise you."

A week later Adam was transferred back out of the freezer, and a week after that he started his call with, "Mom, somebody else died." His voice was full of sorrow.

"What happened, Adam?"

"Alice was a really sweet woman. She was Native American and about 50 years old. She had been working on this boat for ten years." He sighed. "On Friday she told the foreman she didn't feel well and wanted to be flown back to the Mainland. But the foreman said she couldn't go back unless she paid the thousand dollars to be airlifted out. I guess she didn't have the money so she didn't leave." His voice broke. "But Sunday, they found her dead! She had died of a heart attack, and that's why she hadn't been feeling well. If only they had let her fly back …"

I didn't know this woman, so my grief wasn't visceral like Adam's, but I was angry. How little did they care about human life? And the question I kept asking myself—would Adam survive?

The ship was to pull out of the harbor and sail the Bering Sea for a month. No more ship-to-shore calls. I was scared.

Shortly after his last call, as I was praying for him, I was compelled by the Spirit to pray that his shipmates would not murder him! I was taken aback by this moving of the Spirit because it hadn't crossed my mind that his shipmates might kill him.

As a result, for the whole month—morning, noon, and night—I was on my knees before the Lord with this request.

Just over a month after his last call, Adam called from Seattle. "Mom, my contract is up and they flew me to Seattle."

After a pause, his voice became serious and he said, "You won't believe what happened three days ago."

"Try me."

"There's this one guy, Tony. He got mad for no reason. He came up to me while I was doing the breaking job and said to me, 'I'm gonna kill you! With a knife!' See, recently on another one of our company's fishing boats a man was knifed to death, so I took his threat seriously."

"What did you do?"

"There was nothing I could do. I just kept working. They don't allow you to stop.

"But then Tony went up to my lead and told her that he was going to kill me!"

"Whoever does that?" I said. "If you're going to kill somebody, you just do it! You don't announce it to the boss first."

I wondered if Tony told the boss as a result of my prayers.

"So what happened?" I asked.

"My lead came up to me and told me Tony planned to kill me. She said that I'd better watch my back. I told her I knew and I was watching out.

"Believe it or not, the fishing company contacted a rescue helicopter and within 24 hours it flew out to our ship and airlifted Tony to the Mainland!"

Why had they bothered to save Adam? I suspected I knew the answer.

Then I told him how the Lord had moved me a month earlier to pray that his coworkers wouldn't succeed at murdering him, and how I'd been praying fervently all month.

Adam gasped.

We both knew then that nothing would ever happen to him that the Lord didn't allow.

Eventually, Adam worked as a medic in the Army, graduated from college on the G.I. Bill, and began working in a Christian organization where he could use the gifts God has given him and his knowledge of Asia.

GLORIA AND THE CROSS-CULTURAL MARRIAGE PROPOSAL

2010-2011, Re Dai

I looked at my beautiful Chinese friend incredulously. I couldn't believe what I had just heard.

"I want to marry your son Adam," Gloria had said in Mandarin. "Could you give him my phone number? Then he can call me from America, we can get to know each other better and make arrangements for the wedding."

"But you hardly know Adam!" I said. "He only visited here for a few weeks and the two of you weren't together much."

"Oh, that doesn't matter. I know *you*, Grace. I want to marry a son of yours."

That's not the American dream of romance. You like the mother, so you choose her as your mother-in-law, and you want to marry her son whom you hardly know! But that somewhat fits with the *traditional Chinese* view that the bride is marrying into the groom's family hierarchy.

Some Chinese women want to marry American men so they can

immigrate to America, but I knew Gloria had absolutely no interest in leaving China. She was devoting her life to reaching the Chinese in our province with the gospel.

§§§

Gloria and I had first gotten to know each other about six months earlier when Justin and I were invited to the same Chinese tea ceremony as Gloria by a high government official named Russ.

It was an elaborate tea ceremony. When Justin and I arrived at the tea house, we sat opposite Russ at a massive walnut tea table. The table had been artistically carved following the natural contours of the wood. Much of its surface was not flat, but terraced into sweeping curves of mocha-brown. I felt a sense of peace just looking at this aesthetic craftsmanship.

We barely knew Russ. We had accepted his invitation because we hoped to get to know him better. But instead of talking with us, Russ pulled out his phone and started inviting more and more people to the tea. Russ was a nationally famous poet. As soon as he finished making calls, he busied himself writing passionate poems about China which he then read to us so we could compliment them. We never got a chance to converse with him. He wasn't interested in friendship, with us or anyone else for that matter. He just wanted to show off how many friends he had, how lavishly he could entertain, and how skillfully he could write poetry. The more we got to know him, the less interested we were in knowing him.

Gloria was sitting catty-corner to me at the tea table. She held herself with poise, and her clothes had the casual elegance of wealth. I shrank slightly under the table to hide my bargain shirt. I had liked my shirt, but looking at her I now realized how cheap it looked. But she didn't seem to notice my clothes—she only saw me, and it was obvious she was dying to engage me in conversation.

After more of Russ' friends arrived, the tea ceremony began. The woman who was professionally employed as the tea server was dressed in a traditional Chinese red silk dress. She was silent, deep in concentration as she poured water into the teapot, her elbow repeatedly lifting to head height in slow sweeping motions. To produce the desired flavor, each variety of tea was rinsed a set number of times and steeped for a precise number of seconds before being poured into our two-tablespoon-capacity preheated cups.

As soon as we started sipping the subtle flavors of the first cup of tea, Gloria engaged me in conversation in Mandarin. She couldn't stop talking about her love for the Lord. She told me how she and her mother hadn't known anything about God, but through the witness of a friend they had come to believe in Jesus eight years earlier.

I couldn't believe she had the temerity in this public setting to talk so freely about the Lord, especially in front of a high government official.

At the end of the night, we exchanged phone numbers as we were both anxious to see more of each other.

When I invited her over, we sat down in my living room and talked over a cup of ordinary tea. Gloria worked at the two jade stores her family owned in the old section of town near the Confucian temple. Her family also owned a number of houses and plots of land. They were extremely successful capitalists in this newly capitalist country. Gloria was probably the wealthiest person I ever became friends with in China.

I knew from our first meeting how much Gloria loved Jesus, but she shared with me how difficult it was for her to follow him. Her father was very angry that she and her mom had become Christians. In fact, he had forbidden her mom to go to church, and that put Gloria in a tough spot.

"As a good Chinese daughter, I need to respect and obey my father—you know, filial piety—but it's important that my mother attend church so she can grow as a Christian. It's been a terrible dilemma for me—should I obey my father or bring my mother to fellowship with other believers? So I compromise and once a month I sneak my mother out of the house and take her to church. I make sure my father never finds out!"

Filial piety—the obedience, respect, and care due one's parents and the older generation—is an important traditional value for the Chinese, and it stems from the Confucian influence on the culture. It can include love for parents and ancestors, but not necessarily. What's most important is that the child treat the parents properly according to

Confucian ideals, regardless of any love or lack of it. In the younger generation filial piety is waning, but for Gloria it was a critical aspect of how she lived out her walk with Jesus, even though it's fundamentally a Confucian concept.[38] That was why bringing her mother to church was such a moral conflict for her—it pitted the Confucian way she was following the Lord against her mother's need for Christian fellowship.

§§§

A couple months after we met, Gloria and I started making plans to share the gospel as a team to the Chinese people in our province. As our first step, we decided to invite Russ, the high government official, to our home for a barbeque.

We sat on our large, outdoor, private porch, and after we had finished eating barbequed chicken wings and pork chops, Gloria sat back and asked Russ if he had ever thought about God.

Russ answered, "No. Why would I think about someone who doesn't exist?"

I spoke to him in Mandarin, "When you walked into our apartment, you passed by the kitchen with its stove, sink, exhaust fan, and refrigerator. You saw the bathroom with its toilet, sink, and bathtub, and you saw the whole layout of our apartment and its furniture. Would you assume all of that came about by chance?"

"Of course not," he replied.

"And why not?" I asked. I waited but he didn't say anything because he had never thought about such practical things—he was just regurgitating what he'd been indoctrinated into. I was going to have to do some of this lightweight thinking for him. "You know it couldn't have come about by chance because it's so complex, plus it serves a function. It's the same with the trees out there." I pointed to the trees visible from our porch and explained some of their biological complexity, from the xylem and phloem to the amazing function of chlorophyll. "So it's obvious that not only are trees complex, but their complexity serves a function. That speaks of them having been

---

[38] There is overlap between filial piety and the biblical honoring of parents, but filial piety seems to primarily value external behavior.

designed, not having come about by chance."

Afterward, Russ told us that he had never thought about these things before and he wanted more opportunities to talk with us about God!

Gloria and I were very successful as a team in sharing about the Lord—she knew how to start the conversation and I knew how to continue it. I also realized that, because Gloria was so wealthy and respected, I had protection in talking about the Lord, even with a high official. The discussion with Gloria and Russ at the barbeque was the first time I had ever dared to share Jesus with a high government official.

§§§

Before Gloria knew about Adam, she told me how difficult it was to find a husband. "A number of men have wanted to marry me." She sighed. "And my father, he's been trying to match me up with rich young men. They're all nice, but I only want to marry a devoted Christian."

In mid-December, when I told her I had an unmarried son and he was going to fly from America to visit us over Christmas, her eyes lit up. She offered to drive me to the airport—a ten-hour round trip. That should have been a clue for me, but I never dreamed she would want to marry my son sight unseen! When she came to pick me up she was dressed in a crimson suit, even more classy than usual, and she had brought a large bouquet of flowers to give to Adam.

After we arrived at the airport when I spotted Adam coming out of the arrivals gate, I ran up to him with a cry of joy. Face full of love, he wrapped his arms around me. I didn't realize that Adam's affection for me was a turn-on for Gloria. She interpreted his love for me to be filial piety, which she later told me was one of the main qualifications she was looking for in a husband.

During Adam's visit almost every day Gloria invited the two of us to do fun things with her. We spent a day exploring a cave filled with stalactites and stalagmites, but otherwise we turned down all her invitations.

Finally, the day before Adam returned to the States, Gloria called and said she had to see Adam because she had bought him a present—a pair of real Nikes. Real Nikes were very hard to find in China and cost hundreds of U.S. dollars. The knock-off Nikes that were sold everywhere were cheaply made, and after a couple weeks of wear, the soles might fall off.

When Adam tried the shoes on, they were exactly his size.

A week later, when she came over to visit, she told me how she had figured out Adam's shoe size.

"I knew that Thursday evening your family would be out, so I sat in my car for hours near your home waiting for your family to return so Adam's shoes would be outside your door." She had noticed that we followed the Chinese custom of leaving our shoes outside the door when we entered our home.

"After you returned, I stood outside the locked gate of your stairwell in the cold rain until an old man opened the gate to leave, so I could slip inside. I measured one of Adam's shoes because I don't know anything about American sizes, and I bought Nikes with those same measurements!"

Hearing this story, I finally realized what was going on. Gloria was in love with Adam, and I was also beginning to suspect that she had never fallen in love before.

Traditionally in China, marriage was just a contract between a man and a woman simply for the purpose of having children. Knowing each other intimately, enjoying interesting conversation or a good laugh—these were all secondary. After the wedding, it was a bonus if the couple grew to like each other, but what was essential was that they provide progeny who would take care of the living ancestors and worship the ones who had passed away.

But the younger, modern generation is much more interested in falling in love, and having a close, intimate relationship with their spouse. Gloria was a curious combination of both the ancient and modern thinking about marriage.

The next time she came to visit, she couldn't stop talking about Adam, and she asked me to tell him to call her so they could arrange the wedding. I emphasized that I couldn't tell Adam he should call her, that would be his decision. But that didn't seem to faze her. In that area of China many marriages were arranged, and she was sure that, in spite of everything I was saying, not only would I tell Adam to call her, but I would also tell him he was to marry her.

When she got ready to leave that evening, she grabbed me and hugged me in what was a huge embrace for someone with her delicate figure. She had never hugged me before and she didn't let go for about a minute. In her mind, she was hugging her future mother-in-law.

I didn't know how to slow this train down. I wasn't sure whether Adam would contact her or not, but I knew he wouldn't want to be told who he was going to marry.

A few days later I called Adam and told him what Gloria had in mind. He said, "But Mom, I can't support a wife. I don't even have a career yet."

When I relayed his response to Gloria, she said, "That doesn't matter. He doesn't need a career because I have a lot of money and I own a house. We'll live in my house and he won't have to work. We'll spend our time traveling around this province together sharing the gospel."

When I told Adam her plan, he said, "But Mom, she's made all the plans and decided everything for my life. What about me? What about what I want? I don't want to just fit into her plans. She's beautiful and I like her, but that's not enough. She doesn't speak any English at all, and even though I speak Mandarin, my Mandarin isn't good enough for a marriage relationship. And she doesn't want to come to America, even for a visit. How would she ever know my culture, and if she doesn't know my culture, how could she ever really know me?"

I wanted to break it to her slowly. A couple of weeks later I asked her, "Gloria, has Adam called yet?"

She looked both hopeful and sad. "Not yet, but I'm sure he will."

"Gloria, if Adam doesn't call, you won't be able to marry him."

Every few weeks I asked her again if Adam had called. But he never called.

Gloria looked more and more sad. After about six months she told me in a flat voice, "There's a man from Zao Gao City who's interested in me, and he came to see me. His name is Matt. He's a Christian and he's working for a Christian charity."

"That's great, Gloria. It's so hard to find a Christian man to marry, especially one who's serving the Lord. Do you like him?"

"He's OK. But I'm not interested in him. I want to marry Adam."

"But Gloria, Adam never called. You're not going to be able to marry Adam."

"But I'm not interested in anyone else."

A couple of months later when Gloria came over for a visit, she told me, "Matt asked me to marry him, but I'm not that interested in him. And I can't figure out what I want."

"Do you have anything in common?"

"Other than serving the Lord, filial piety toward our parents is the most important thing to each of us."

I would have hoped they would have had more in common, but I asked, "Have you prayed about the decision?"

"Of course, but I can't marry someone I'm not interested in."

"OK, let's settle this once and for all." I walked over to a cabinet and pulled out a one-yuan coin. "Heads—you marry Matt. Tails—you don't."

I flipped the coin. Tails.

"So how do you feel?" I asked.

"A little sad."

I flipped the coin again. Heads.

"How do you feel?"

"Kind of happy."

"Well, now you know your feelings. You do have some desire to marry him."

A few months later Justin and I joyfully attended Gloria and Matt's wedding. They shared the gospel at their wedding and are still sharing the gospel together in their province.

THE GOSPEL—DORMANT FOR 75 YEARS!

2009-2012, Re Dai

The first time I visited Wayne, my new 85-year-old friend, he told me he had been a logistics coordinator for the Flying Tigers during the Anti-Japanese War. His wrinkled face flashed an impish smile at me. "I think the Anti-Japanese War is what you Americans call World War II, is that right?"

We were sitting in the ten-by-ten-foot living room of his apartment in this home for the elderly. He sat catty-corner to me in a straight-back wooden chair, and I sat in the center sag of his two-person couch, continuously shifting my butt because of how uncomfortable the couch was. A small pink-flowered blanket covered the middle of it, partially hiding its shabbiness.

"Do you know who the Flying Tigers were?" he asked.

"They were the American Air Force pilots who saved this province from the Japanese after America joined the war, right?"

"Not exactly. This was before Pearl Harbor, and the American government didn't want to start an official all-out war with Japan, so the pilots ..." he gestured, ripping off a lapel. "They pretended they were civilian pilots, even though they were American military."

So the American Air Force had fought against Japan clandestinely *before* Pearl Harbor? I had thought we hadn't started fighting Japan until *after* Pearl Harbor!

I studied Wayne more closely—his thin wisps of gray hair, overly large ears, prominent bony cheekbones, and square jaw on his too-thin face. One of his eyes was blind, clouded over with a cataract, and the other eye was partially clouded.

He not only knew events of my country's history that I didn't know, he had even been a part of America's history. And his English! He said all of this in English, and he knew English words I didn't even know. If I spoke to him in Chinese, he always answered in English.

Wayne continued his story. "I grew up in Huangdi. My parents enrolled me in a Christian middle school run by missionaries."

Unexpectedly he burst out singing, "Lord, I want to be a Christian in my heart. Lord, I want to be a Christian in my heart. Lord, I want to be a Christian in my heart."

My eyes widened.

"I learned that song in the missionary school," he said.

He moved on before I could ask him if he truly believed in Jesus and meant what he sang.

"During high school the Japanese invaded Huangdi. We fled to Zao Gao City, just north of here. I was attending college when the Japanese invaded this province, and I was drafted to work for the Flying Tigers."

I was becoming more and more intrigued by this old man.

After relating a few of his experiences with the Flying Tigers, he laughed. "The communists took over in 1949. During the Anti-Rightist Campaign in the late 50s, they wanted to punish anyone who had had anything to do with Americans. Because I had worked for the Flying Tigers, they imprisoned and tortured me for ten years."

Like many older Chinese who relate horrible things that happened to them, he looked impassive and even laughed.

"They made my wife divorce me and my children were lost to me." His eyes narrowed in pain. Then he looked at me kindly.

You would have thought Wayne would have been a national hero. But no, not in a communist country. I had heard stories similar to his, but none so clearly damning the communists' black and white thinking—picking out groups of people to condemn instead of recognizing people individually for their character and contributions. In this case the people chosen for condemnation had even helped save China.

I wondered about Wayne's willingness to become friends with me, an American. Was I a danger to him? I asked him why he was willing to talk with me.

"It's different now."

I visited him every other week. He was a connoisseur of tea, and for the first half hour of each visit we discussed the tea he served me. "Is this tea grown in the highlands or the lowlands?" "Exactly what time of day do they pick this tea to retain its fullest flavor?" (Usually 10 a.m.) He always told me if the tea was drought-resistant or not, but that was the only English word he couldn't pronounce properly, so it came out "dot-resistant." I never corrected this man I had so much respect for.

Before I would drink the tea, he would ask me to smell its aroma. Was it fragrant? After I took my first sip, we would talk about the flavor. Was it woody? Flowery? Bitter? Sweet?

I had no interest in talking about tea, but he wouldn't have been friends with me if I hadn't discussed his tea with him first. So that's what I did. I was buying the opportunity to talk with him about deeper topics. We would spend the next hour and a half talking about life and the Lord.

On the second visit he told me about an Irish woman who had visited him the year before. "After she and I talked a while, she looked me straight in the eye and said, 'I feel so sorry for you!' I couldn't figure out what she was talking about. I've had a rough life, but things were going pretty good for me then, at age 84. So I asked her why she felt sorry for me, and she said, 'I feel sorry for you because you have lived so long and you still don't know Jesus!'"

What a way to introduce Christ! I'm usually a little more slow, gentle, and subtle.

"She returned to Ireland and I never saw her again."

"So what was your reaction when she said that?" I asked.

"I was offended! See, I was an atheist and I just thought God and

Jesus were myths. But then I got to thinking—a couple decades ago I was in the mountains, and a boulder fell off a mountain right in front of me, missing me by only a few centimeters." He used his fingers to emphasize how close a call it was. "After the Irish woman was here, I came to the conclusion there must be a God because *Someone* had saved my life."

I looked at him expectantly.

"Because of my Christian school background, I decided that the one who spared my life must be the Christian God."

But he had attended the missionary school over 70 years ago! When he never responded to the Lord other than learning to sing their songs, the missionaries must have been disappointed. But here, so many years later, his hearing the gospel as a child was bearing fruit.

He continued, "So I decided I wanted to become a Christian. But I didn't know how and I didn't know any Christians to ask. So I thought and thought about this problem and came up with a plan—I'd go to the Three-Self Church [the government church] and ask someone how to become a Christian."

I was sitting on the edge of my seat.

"I sat through the whole service, but before and after the service not one person talked to me." He looked disgusted. "The pastor didn't even greet me! If *anyone* had spoken to me, I would have asked them how to become a Christian. When I left the church, I was so frustrated—how was I supposed to become a Christian?" He sighed. "I didn't know what to do, so I came home and sat here for several months, wanting to become a Christian but not knowing how."

How tragic! The church had failed him because they weren't friendly.

Then his face brightened. "A few months ago I went to an English corner[39] where I met a Chinese woman, Gloria.[40] Out of the blue she stared at me and asked, 'Do you want to become a Christian?' I was so excited. I told her, 'That's exactly what I want to do!' So she took me to her house church and her pastors baptized me. Isn't that great! I've

---

[39] An English corner is a gathering of Chinese English speakers who want to improve their English through conversation.

[40] This is the Gloria from "Gloria and the Cross-Cultural Marriage Proposal."

finally become a Christian."

I smiled. "That's fantastic!"

He broke into singing, "Lord, I want to be a Christian in my heart."

But I wanted to make sure he really did know the Lord because I had met so many Chinese in that town who claimed to be Christians but didn't know the first thing about Christ. So I asked him, "What did they tell you about Jesus?"

"What? Oh, nothing. They didn't tell me anything about Jesus."

I was becoming alarmed. "What did they tell you about becoming a Christian?"

He looked at me confused. "What are you talking about? I already am a Christian—I was baptized!"

"Wayne, what is a Christian?"

He just stared at me.

"How does a person become a Christian?"

"I don't know!" He looked at me annoyed. "I don't know the answer to all your questions. What I do know is that I'm a Christian because I've been baptized."

Later, when I met Gloria, I found out that she was part of the evangelical house church movement. Why she hadn't explained the gospel but had only had him baptized, I didn't know. But Wayne was a baptized unbeliever. He didn't know the Lord yet.

For months, during every visit, after we discussed the tea, I tried to talk to him about the Lord and the gospel. But he argued and argued with me against the gospel. Often I showed him a few verses of Scripture, but he couldn't understand them, and when he did, he didn't like what they said.

We were making painfully slow progress. *After about a year*, he started to understand that Jesus had died for his sins. But he only partially understood.

At a Christmas dinner, he sat next to me at a large round table with a number of his Chinese friends, many of whom were government officials and policemen. After we finished eating, Wayne stood up, looked around at his friends and announced, "*Jesus will forgive your sins. It doesn't matter whether you're Buddhist or atheist. You don't need to believe in him. He'll forgive your sins because he died for you on the cross.*" Then he sat down again.

I didn't say anything. It wouldn't do for me to contradict him publicly, because in Chinese culture it's so important not to make people lose face. But more important, these government officials and policemen would have noticed if at the dinner I was teaching Wayne about the Lord.

The next time I visited I showed him John 6:35—it's the person who *comes* to Jesus who will never go hungry, and the person who *believes* in Jesus who will never thirst. Then I showed him John 7:37. Whoever is thirsty should *come* and drink from Jesus.

I looked up at Wayne. He nodded. "I see. You have to *come* to get."

The Ching Ming Festival was approaching. It's an important Chinese holiday where everyone travels to the gravesites of their ancestors to worship them, usually to the countryside, or up a mountain. They look like pilgrims—groups of extended family trudging to remote places packed down with a broom for sweeping the grave, incense sticks, offerings of fruit for the dead, and hell money, which they burn in order to transfer the money to the bank accounts of the dead.

Shortly before Ching Ming, I was again enjoying a dinner with Wayne and his friends, this time it was a birthday celebration. Abby,[41] a mutual friend of ours whom I had recently led to the Lord, was on my right and Wayne was seated on my left.

During the meal Abby asked me, "Now that I'm a Christian, can I still worship my ancestors at the Ching Ming Festival?"

I told her that we Christians only worship God, but that she can show respect to her ancestors at their graves. In fact, the Lord wants us to respect our ancestors.

Wayne overheard our conversation. He glared at me. *"Now there's Christianity, and there's Chinese."* His hand chopped in the air two separate spheres of identity. *"We're Chinese so we need to follow the Chinese culture and worship our ancestors at their graves!"*

I didn't say anything. He needed time to cool down before I could talk with him.

---

[41] This is Abby from "The Tree Worshipper" in *Dragon Ride.*

Two weeks later when I visited him, I asked if he had worshipped his ancestors during the Ching Ming Festival.

He answered, "I thought a lot about what you said, and I didn't worship my ancestors."

That was a huge step and I was very excited, but I decided to take it a step farther. I said, "You should tell your relatives that after you die they shouldn't worship you."

"I've already told them!" he said with a big smile. "And not just once. I told them *seven times*!"

I couldn't help but laugh.

Wayne had a lot of trouble believing that the Bible is completely true. Because of his cataracts he couldn't read, so he started listening to tapes of the Bible. After he finished listening to Matthew through Acts he commented, "Well, I didn't like that very much!"

I looked at him in surprise.

He sneered. "Like the story about the five cakes and two fish where Jesus fed those thousands of people. It's just a children's story. It's make-believe. That's not a story for adults, and it shouldn't be in the Bible. I want something more meaty!"

As I listened to him ridiculing what is so precious to me, he wound up for another attack.

"And furthermore, it's just like those stupid made-up Buddhist stories where impossible miracles happen. I had thought the Bible was going to be better than that and have something of content, something worth reading."

I sighed and told him about a disabled Christian friend of mine in New York who didn't have enough money to live on. "But after she paid her bills, when she looked at her bank statement, there was more money in her account than there possibly could have been." I paused to let this sink in. "The Lord made her money grow just like he did the five cakes and two fish. The Lord is capable of doing that. The story about feeding the 5,000 is true, and from my friend's story you can see that it's relevant to us adults."

He looked like he was half convinced.

But later, when I asked him if he thought the Bible was true, he looked disgusted and spit out, "Well, it depends on what it says."

Finally, he looked away and asked, "Do you know what I'm thinking?"

I was confused and didn't say anything.

"I'm wondering when you're going to leave."

I sat frozen for a minute. He was always lively and feisty, but I had never seen him rude like this before. He was kicking me out!

Then he faced me. "I'm tired of hearing about the Bible. I don't want to hear it anymore."

I stood up, gathered my things, said goodbye and left.

And I didn't go back, but I kept praying for him.

Five weeks later he called. "Grace, please come back!" He frequently spoke in metaphors. "I'm a horse who needs grass. The Bible is the grass—I'm so hungry for it. Please come back and teach me the Bible!" The Lord had been using the time while I was gone to make him hungry for the Scriptures.

I started visiting him again, discussing tea and the Bible, but something had changed in him—he was no longer angrily fighting against the Bible; instead, he was now running toward it and he finally started to understand it. A few months later he told me that whenever I explained the Bible to him it was like receiving a revelation from God.

Many Chinese people believe in reincarnation. I didn't know if Wayne did or not, so one day I showed him Hebrews 9:27, that we die only once and then we'll be judged. I emphasized that we are not reincarnated.

His face broke into a huge grin. He laughed. "I knew it! I figured out that reincarnation was wrong thirty years ago, because even one life is too hard to live!" It strengthened his faith in the Bible, realizing that it taught something he had already come to believe was true.

For three years, until we moved from that town, every other week I visited him. Slowly, very slowly, he started to grasp the gospel.

Finally, after he had fully come to faith, he announced one day, "I only have one photon of God, but no more."

I couldn't figure out what he was talking about.

He continued, "There are a lot of people who believe in God, so there's not enough of God to spread around. So each person who believes in him gets only one photon of him."

I showed him John 14:23. I said, "God makes his home in everyone who loves him, and God can fully live in everyone who believes in him because he's so great."

It was a completely new thought to him, but it filled him with joy that he had more than one photon of God.

One afternoon I was talking with Wayne about my intimacy with God, and I told him something I had never shared with anyone before because I thought people would think I was proud. "Wayne, I feel like God loves me real special. I feel funny saying that because there are a lot of Christians. Why would he love me so specially?"

Wayne's eyes got big. "You feel that way, too? I feel like God loves me like I'm his only child—I'm that special to him."

I looked off into the distance. "Maybe every believer feels like they are exceptionally precious to the Lord. I hadn't realized that."

§§§

To decorate his living room, on one wall Wayne had pasted a lot of pictures of fruit he had cut out of magazines. It made him happy to look at the fruit.

On another wall were pictures of people from a part of China who had lived well past 100, even up to 124 years old. He loved telling me what contributed to them living so long; usually it was the water they drank.

But when I visited him one afternoon I saw a new decoration on the third wall—he had made a clock out of construction paper. Above the clock was a picture of four grade school kids looking expectantly over a wall. He had placed them so they looked like they were watching the clock. I asked him about it.

"The numbers on the clock are my age. The kids are all excited to see how old I get." Then he told me about the division of responsibility between him and God. "It's my responsibility to take care of my health so I'll live to 90. After that, keeping me alive is God's responsibility!"

He told me that God kept him alive so long so he could come to know him.

Tears came to my eyes. I was so glad for Wayne's young faith.

There's a Chinese saying, *nan de hu du.* (I was wise all my life, but then I did one thing that was really stupid.) After he came to know the Lord, Wayne changed the saying to *nan de cong ming.* (I was stupid all my life, but then I finally did something smart.) He told me that the one smart thing he did was believe in Jesus. He wrote his new saying in large Chinese characters on a piece of construction paper and fastened it to the fourth wall, which could be easily seen from the hallway of his retirement home. "That way I can tell everyone who passes by about the one smart thing I did in life."

After he turned 90, I asked Wayne if he was afraid of being persecuted for being a Christian. He laughed and said, "I've been persecuted a lot in my life. But I'm 90 years old. What can they do to me now? Of course, I'm not afraid!"

At the time of this writing, Wayne is 97 years old and still going strong. He attends church regularly and shares the gospel. He spends every evening from 9 to 9:30 praying and waiting on the Lord. And he's lonely now because I'm not in China anymore. And I'm lonely because I can't visit him now.

The seed of the gospel had been planted in Wayne's heart when he was just 12 years old. He hadn't believed it and hadn't understood it. That seed lay dormant for 75 years! Then, by God's power, it finally sprouted and Wayne came to believe in Jesus at age 87!

BONUS
A GOD BEYOND COMPARISON

In this section

from my experience encountering other religions and beliefs,

I will demonstrate the uniqueness and beauty

of the one true God and the gospel.

I will also explain

what attracted my Buddhist friends to the Christian God.

And throughout

I will give challenges to those of us who know God

and insights about sharing Jesus with those who don't know him.

A GOD BEYOND COMPARISON

Introduction

While I was in the middle of writing this section an American friend whom I had been sharing the Lord with asked what I was writing about. When I told her I was writing what I learned about the Christian God from encountering the Buddhist faith and other faiths, she asked if I had heard the story of the elephant.

She recounted it for me. "There was a Protestant pastor, a Catholic priest, and a Buddhist monk who were all blindfolded and touching different parts of an elephant. One described a mouth, the second said it had a tail, and the third described the toes. Because their descriptions were so different, they thought they were touching different animals, but they were actually describing different parts of the *same* animal." Then she asked, "Isn't that just like the religions of the world? Everyone is worshipping the same god—they just know different aspects of that same god."

I responded, "Maybe the Buddhist monk was touching a *tiger*, not an elephant."

She jarred up. I could tell that by changing the metaphor she was beginning to doubt the "undeniable truth" of her original metaphor.

Then I told her, "I'm writing what I came to understand about the elephant by contrasting it with the tiger."

The illustration my friend told me is a parable from India which has convinced many people around the world that all religions are essentially the same, the gods people worship are all the same god, and that each religion is just a different path to reach this god.

It's a powerful illustration in many ways and seemingly solves one of the great mysteries of life. But the problem with the illustration is that it presupposes what it's trying to prove—*that they all were touching the same animal.*

Before living in Asia and becoming close friends with people of other faiths, I just assumed that even though other gods were not the same being as the Christian God, they would nevertheless be very similar to him in character—they would be righteous, moral, just, loving, merciful, and forgiving. And they would be concerned with our spiritual and moral development. I mean, who would want to worship a god who isn't as good as that?

To think that all religions are basically the same and all gods are the same is an easy mistake to make if you haven't become close friends with people of other faiths—if you haven't lived in their home culture and seen them practice their faith; and if you aren't fluent in their mother tongue, discussing their religion with them in their heart language. In other words, thinking that all religions and gods are the same is just a theoretical assumption. It is not based on the reality of practical experience of other religions.

This section is very personal for me because while living in Asia, not only did I come to realize how unique and amazingly beautiful the Christian God is, but this awareness has energized my worship of him.

A GOD BEYOND COMPARISON

Part 1

Idol Worship/Chinese Folk Religion

Understanding idol worship was what most profoundly impressed on me the uniqueness of our God.

When I was studying Cantonese in Hong Kong, my professor told the class this story: "A shop owner went to the temple of the god, Wong Tai Sin. He offered money to the idol and prayed that his business would be protected from vandals.

"After he left, a *thief* came into the temple and offered the idol *even more money* than the shop owner did. He prayed that Wong Tai Sin would *help him steal from the store of the shop owner who had just left the temple.*"

Then my professor asked, "Who will Wong Tai Sin help—the shop owner or the thief? Both gave him an offering and asked him to help them thwart the request of the other."

After a pause, she said, "*Of course he'll help the thief steal from the shop owner because the thief gave him more money than the shop owner did.* You see, the idol is just mercenary. He doesn't care about the shop owner or the thief. His powers are for sale to the biggest donor—he's selfish, he just loves money."

My mind immediately went to the contrasts with the Christian God. Do we have to pay God so he will help us? Is our God selfish?

One of the main roles idols play in many Hong Kong people's lives is to give them what they ask for. But our God is not a genie whose sole purpose is to give us everything we want. That would be a pretty thin relationship.

Furthermore, the Hong Kong gods work on a quid pro quo basis—you have to give them something in order to get favors from them. But our God doesn't sell his favors—Jesus never accepted any payment for healing people. And when Simon the Sorcerer tried to buy the ability to dispense the Holy Spirit, Peter rebuked him harshly (Acts 8:18-23). (Also see II Kings 5:8-27.)

What follows from that is that because idols require expensive gifts commensurate with their services, the poor have no one to help them; only the rich are helped by an idol. Not so the true God. Because he deeply loves the people he created, he helps us with our needs, and he *especially* helps those who can't help themselves, who are the ones who have little to offer him. This is even more true in the spiritual area, where he helps those who are spiritually needy if they recognize their need (Matthew 5:3; Mark 2:17).

In two clear examples we see the Lord's extra kindness to the poor and how he valued the small gift they offered him. The Old Testament's required offering after the birth of a child was adjusted for poverty. "But if she cannot afford a lamb, she is to bring two doves or two young pigeons ..." (Leviticus 12:8). The Lord was happy with an inexpensive, commonplace offering the poor could afford. The Lord's pleasure in the small gifts of the poor is also obvious when Jesus praised the poor widow for putting only two small coins into the treasury (Mark 12:41-44). Christianity is completely different from many of the world's religions where an expensive offering is the way to buy favor from a deity.

I've seen a perversion of Christianity that looks to me like idol worship. It's where you give money to a "Christian" preacher so that God will grant your wishes. Or you give a seed offering to get favors from God. Not only are these practices similar to idol worship, they are totally contrary to the beautiful character of the true God, who freely gives us good things because he loves us (Matthew 7:9-11). The Christian God never sells his blessings.

Moral vs. Amoral

It's natural for Christians to think that all gods would be moral because we're used to the character of the true God. I was quite surprised to encounter gods who couldn't have cared less about right and wrong.

Wong Tai Sin in the professor's story wasn't interested in morality. He was just as willing to help the thief steal as he was to protect the shop owner from the thief, depending on who gave him more money.

But being concerned about right and wrong is core to the character of the Christian God. This goes beyond caring if an action is right or wrong; the Lord is actively working for our moral development. This means that he doesn't always give us everything we want because that would turn us into self-centered, demanding, materialistic people. He also doesn't answer requests that come from a greedy heart to satisfy unrighteous desires (James 4:3).

Instead, God is our parent. He sees the bigger picture of how we are maturing, so he disciplines us in ways that will produce righteousness and peace, even if it temporarily hurts (Hebrews 12:5-11). This is completely different from how idols deal with people.

Close vs. Distant

Hong Kong idol worshippers don't draw close to their gods in what we would consider a satisfying personal relationship. There's a Chinese saying, "Stay as far away as you can from the king and the gods." In other words, placate them by giving them what they require so they won't hurt you, but don't be close to them!

In contrast, the Lord longs for intimate personal relationship with us (Jeremiah 30:21b-22; Revelation 3:20). In fact, the core goal of the Christian faith is to find forgiveness in Jesus so we can be close to God, grow in our knowledge of him, and please him.

As we see what the Hong Kong gods are like in contrast to how concerned our God is about our moral character, how close he wants to be to us, and how generous and loving he is, especially to the helpless, it becomes clear that we're not all worshipping the same god.

"Among the gods there is none like you, Lord ..." (Psalm 86:8).

I have so much more appreciation for the God I serve after coming to understand the gods of this world, and this has strengthened my worship of him. Psalm 35:10 says, "My whole being will exclaim, 'Who is like you, LORD? You rescue the poor from those too strong for them, the poor and needy from those who rob them.'" When I read verses like this, my heart soars in praise to our great God because I know what a beautiful God I serve.

A Few Thoughts About Sharing Jesus

Most of us don't personally know an idol worshipper. But many of us know someone who shares an aspect of the beliefs of an idol worshipper, especially the quid pro quo aspect, that we need to give something to a deity in order to get something from that deity. It's a very human belief to think that we have to earn or be worthy of what we're given, and that's the basic premise of almost all religions.

We notice this quid pro quo more easily if the gift is monetary. But good works can serve this function, too—as when someone offers good works to gain entrance into paradise/heaven or to gain favor with God or a deity. Christianity is unique in that through faith and repentance we, who are undeserving, can receive the free gift of salvation and all the blessings that come with it.

My Chinese friends, who were trying to earn their "salvation" by good works, found this aspect of the Christian God very appealing, especially if they had already come to realize that they couldn't possibly reach the goal of being good enough.

§§§

I have discovered that asking my friends what they believe tends to make them receptive to hearing about the Lord. When I listen to them talk about their faith, they feel respected. I show appreciation for the good aspects of their beliefs, and I try to see their faith through their eyes. What I am especially attuned to is what they love about their faith—these are indicators of their deepest longings. Then I ask myself, "How can Christ better satisfy these longings?" I use similarities and contrasts between their beliefs and Christianity to bring out aspects of the Christian faith that may be appealing to them. There are often connections between what is good in their beliefs and Christianity, and there are often telling contrasts between what is unsatisfying in their faith and what the true God has to offer.

I believe the human heart is searching for its creator, the Christian God. This search has been muddied by all sorts of sin, other priorities, distractions, false gods and beliefs. But it is the true God who fully satisfies the heart. This makes me confident in sharing about Jesus.

A GOD BEYOND COMPARISON

Part 2

Buddhism

Many of us in the West know someone who is Buddhist—there are many Asian Buddhist immigrants, and there are a number of non-Asian Westerners who now claim Buddhism as their religion. As a result, Buddhism and its ideas have permeated Western culture, with a lot of Westerners being influenced by Buddhist concepts such as *karma* or *reincarnation*.

This chapter will discuss Asian Buddhism.[42] There are many variations of Asian Buddhism, but I will focus mainly on the Buddhism my friends believed, which has a lot of overlap with other Asian Buddhist beliefs and practices.

To have a framework for understanding Buddhism, it's important to know the story of its founder, Siddhartha Gautama (who was the

---

[42] *Leaving Buddha: A Tibetan Monk's Encounter with the Living God* by Tenzin Lahkpa and Eugene Bach (New Kensingtion, PA: Whitaker House, 2019). The author gives an account of a Tibetan Buddhist monk who left Tibetan Buddhism to become a Christian. He reveals Tibetan Buddhism from an insider's perspective.

Buddha). This story is the foundation of Buddhism, but Buddhists aren't concerned whether this story is true or myth.[43] Gautama grew up as a prince and was very wealthy. His father wanted to protect him from the harsh realities of the world, so he confined him to the palace, and only let him see health, abundance, and youth. But Siddhartha Gautama wanted to experience the world, so he succeeded in escaping the confines of the palace. Once outside the palace grounds, he saw much suffering—disease, poverty, and old age—and it shook him to the core, so he decided he needed to find a solution to the suffering in the world. (So eliminating suffering is the raison d'etre of Buddhism.) Gautama left his wife and son in order to find the answer. (Detachment from the people you love is highly valued in Buddhism.) Through meditation and deprivation, Gautama came to the conclusion that both suffering and this material world are, in fact, not real; they are an illusion caused by attachment to this world and its desires. Coming to this realization and detaching from the world was how Gautama entered the state of nirvana.

The goal of Buddhism, then, is to enter the state of nirvana by realizing that this world and all its pain is just an illusion, and by no longer desiring or being attached to the world.

Nirvana is not what we think of when we think of heaven. Nirvana is the state of being an undifferentiated one with the universe, where there are no emotions, passions, desires, or individuality. It is perfectly peaceful, with no suffering.

Until a person reaches nirvana, he has to remain in the cycle of reincarnation. So reincarnation, in essence, is the punishment for not having entered nirvana. Everyone's station in life, whether good or bad, is the result of how they lived their previous life. So according to Buddhism, women, the disabled, and the poor *in their previous lives* were worse than men, the fully abled, and the rich; and in *this* life they are working off the bad karma or bad deeds from their *previous* lives. This doesn't result in much sympathy for another person's plight in life because they're merely receiving the just punishment for their karma.

[43] Buddhism is not based on the historicity of the Buddha, but rather on the philosophy derived from his life, unlike Christianity which stands or falls with the historicity of Jesus.

That's Buddhism 101, so you can better understand how unique and beautiful Christianity is in comparison to Buddhism and how attractive Christianity can be to a Buddhist.

In talking with a Buddhist friend, it's important to understand what he or she actually believes, not just what Buddhism teaches, although understanding what Buddhism teaches can help because it gives you a framework for understanding what your friend might say. In fact, if I had not first read about Buddhism before talking with my Buddhist friends, I wouldn't have had a clue what they were talking about or how to respond.

Throughout these comparisons between Buddhism and Christianity I will explain what turned the Chinese people I was friends with away from Buddhism and toward Christianity. Seeing what aspects of Christianity resonated with my Buddhist friends may give you ideas and principles for sharing the gospel, both with your Buddhist and non-Buddhist friends.

The Material World and Relationships

The Buddhist and the Christian have very different views of the physical world and our relationship to it. Whereas the Buddhist denies the material world exists, and thinks that our attachment to it is the cause of our painful existence and the reason why we have not yet reached nirvana, Christians embrace the world and view it as the creative expression of God's nature and the object of his love.

Christians also have a deep understanding that this present world is temporary, it is not our permanent home. So for Christians, there is an appreciation of this world, but not a final attachment.

After one Chinese friend turned away from Buddhism and embraced the Lord, he made the observation that the Christian view is very positive and affirms this material world, without clinging to it, but the core of Buddhism is negative and disparages the world we live in.

This Buddhist detachment from the world also influences the Buddhist's attitude toward interpersonal relationships. According to Buddhism, it's not only this world that is transient and not important, but human relationships are also transient and not important.

Relationships cause us to form attachments to people and therefore prevent us from entering nirvana, just like attachment to the world prevents us from reaching nirvana. A Buddhist must break all attachment to people.

For Christians interpersonal relationships are vitally important to our faith. The second most important commandment is that we are to love others as ourselves (Matthew 22:39); we cannot even love God unless we love others (I John 4:20-21); and as Christians we are to fellowship in community, the church, if we are to grow well in our faith (Ephesians 4:11-16; Hebrews 10:24-25).

So Buddhism shuns interpersonal relationships whereas Christianity embraces them.

Suffering

A Chinese friend of mine told me that when he's in pain Buddhism tells him that he's not hurting, that his pain is an illusion—it's all in his head. According to Buddhism, if he would just realize that he's not suffering, then he wouldn't have a problem. He told me that he doesn't find that very comforting when he's hurting. He said that in contrast to Buddhism, Christianity affirms his suffering, tells him there's purpose in it, and that he can grow from it. He added that the Buddhist answer isn't helpful at all. It's the Christian perspective that gives him hope and purpose.

Buddhism denies the existence of suffering; Christianity embraces suffering and teaches us how to grow from it (Hebrews 12:5-11; James 1:2-4).

Desires, Emotions, Personality, and Demeanor

According to Buddhism, *all desires* are bad because they attach us to this world, keep us in the cycle of reincarnation, and prevent us from entering nirvana.

This point was instrumental to a group of Chinese college students I was leading in discussion because I told them that all their good, natural desires were bad according to Buddhism. Since they knew that wasn't true, they walked away from the Buddhist teachings.

Christianity has a more nuanced view—it differentiates between good and evil desires, which fits with how we experience life. Second Peter 1:4 says that the corruption in the world is caused by *evil desires*. James 1:14 says that we are tempted when we are dragged away by our own *evil desires* and enticed. But *good desires* should be satisfied (Psalm 37:4; 103:5; 145:16, 19). And God made everything for us to enjoy (I Timothy 6:17).

One of the first things I noticed when I met a group of orthodox Buddhists was how detached and expressionless they looked. When I actually got to know them, I found that they were full of the jealousies and pride common to mankind, but because their goal was to be devoid of desires or emotions, frankly, their faces looked blah.

In contrast, when you meet a Christian who is growing in the Lord and full of the Holy Spirit, you often quickly notice how alive he is (Psalm 19:7-8; 34:5). Our youngest son, Adam, made use of this in 2003 when he tried to start a Bible study at his college in America. In order to keep the Christians from meeting, the administration was preventing him from advertising the group. Finally, in order to find Christians on campus to invite to the study, he stood in the quad one afternoon and studied the faces of the students who walked by. The ones who glowed with an internal beauty and joy he invited to the study, and he guessed right—they were the Christians! He was able to start the Bible study in spite of the administration blocking him from advertising because it was so obvious who the Christians were.

If Christians are walking well with the Lord, the beauty of their faith often shows on their faces, just as a Buddhist, who is making progress in Buddhism, is distinguished by the lack of emotional expression on his face.

The Christian God values human emotions. In fact, prayer is a very emotional experience for Christians. Our prayer book, the Psalms, overflows with passionate emotion. And the example we have of Jesus is of one who poured out his heart to God in prayer with loud cries and tears (Hebrews 5:7).

Buddhism devalues and dulls much of what makes us human, including personality. After I became a Christian, unexpectedly, the more I came to know the Lord and the closer I got to him, the more my personality came alive. I became more creative and expressive. This makes perfect sense since God created my personality. His goal is not the obliteration of me, but rather the full expression of what he created. Deeper connection with the source of personality brings out personality. I often say: "The more of the Lord, the more of me."[44]

This was very important in attracting one Buddhist friend to Christ. She was accustomed to Buddhism eliminating her personality. When I told her that the closer I am to the Lord, the more my personality blossoms, she became so attracted to Christianity.

Personal God vs. Impersonal Force

When I became acquainted with Buddhists in Mainland China, I noticed a difference between how they feel in the world and how I feel in the world. I feel loved and connected in this world because the creator of the universe cares about me.

If a Buddhist has any concept of a supreme god at all, it is a god that is not relational, has no personality or emotions, and it certainly does not have any love for humans. It's more like a force that functions according to principles than a person. So the Buddhist has a lonely, isolated existence; there's no one looking out for him.

Christianity is personal—it's about developing a relationship with our creator God. This often surprised and attracted the Chinese people I shared Christ with because Buddhism is a philosophy to believe and a state of mind to attain to, not a relationship with one's creator.

Karma and Justice

In America many people love to use the word *karma* in a playful or joking way. But when my Buddhist friends used the word, they usually spoke it with dread—primarily it referred to the bad deeds that they would suffer for.

---

[44] In John 3:30, John the Baptist states: "He must become greater; I must become less." This is referring to Jesus' ministry increasing at the expense of John the Baptist's ministry. It does not refer to any diminishing of John's personality.

In some ways karma seems like a perfectly just system of getting what you deserve—you are punished for the bad you do and rewarded for your good deeds.

And my Buddhist friends made clear to me that there is no mercy in Buddhism. According to Buddhism, there is a celestial scale of justice that metes out punishment and rewards precisely according to your deeds. It's frightening!

The Christian God shows mercy—no matter how he judges people in this life, he loves us, wants to draw us to the light, and he's merciful (John 3:16; II Peter 3:9b; I Timothy 2:4). It pains the Lord when he has to punish us (Jeremiah 48). God doesn't give us what we deserve (Psalm 103:10), and his mercy triumphs over judgment (James 2:13b). Of course, this is seen most clearly in Jesus' substitutionary atonement.

One of my Buddhist friends had tried and tried to get rid of the guilt she felt for her past sins through practicing Buddhism. But Buddhism doesn't provide any solution for sin, so her guilt remained. When she heard that Christ had paid the punishment for her sins she was overwhelmed with joy. Finally, it was through Jesus that she was able to get free from the guilt that had plagued her.

Motivation for Good Works

One day a Buddhist friend emphasized to me that the motivation for being a good person is to avoid punishment. I used this to bring her around to Christ. We had already talked about the two most important biblical injunctions, so I asked her to tell them to me. She replied, "Love God and love people." I said, "If a person does good merely because they fear the punishment their bad karma would bring, that person is acting in self-interest. That's the Buddhist way. But if a person's motivation to do good is because they love God and other people, they're doing good for the sake of others. That's the Christian way. It's the better way." My friend was taken aback and this discussion was instrumental in her coming to faith in Jesus.

A Few More Thoughts About Sharing Jesus

What was helpful for me in sharing Christ with my Buddhist friends is that Christianity fits not just how I experience life, but how they experienced life. My Buddhist friends were generally dissatisfied with the answers to life that Buddhism provided, but the answers Christianity gave rang true in their deepest being. Christianity satisfies the heart's longings.

Actually, with whomever I share about the Lord, this is one of my most powerful, convincing cases for Christianity that attracts my unbelieving friends—Christianity is true to life and answers life's needs and yearnings. And that is why, if I am to witness effectively, I need a close walk with the Lord so that through my life my friends can see what knowing Jesus and living out the gospel looks like.

Christianity fits life because it's true. No other belief system or religion I have encountered fits life so well. Of course it would be this way because the Christian God is the creator of our lives. He designed life, so he knows what brings joy, health, and peace to our hearts.

A GOD BEYOND COMPARISON

Part 3

Marxism

Some aspects of Christianity became so much more liberating to me from our 19 years of living in what was officially a Marxist state, and from knowing Chinese people who had been persecuted under Marxism. We lived in China during a historic time—at the beginning of our stay, the country was basically functioning according to Marxism, but then it transitioned to being fairly capitalistic while retaining its political totalitarianism. It made this change because communist economics weren't working. In order to save face, the Chinese government called this combination "Socialism with Chinese Characteristics."

Many books have been written about Marxism, but I will just share a few things my Chinese friends and I observed while living in China, and I will show how beautiful Christianity is in contrast to Marxism. In this chapter I'll use the word *Marxism* (马克思主义) because in Mainland China that is what the philosophy is called.

Although Marxism isn't officially a religion and it has no god, it does have a heaven, albeit a heaven on earth—a materialistic utopia where there is no private property, and goods are equally dispensed. This is the official goal of Marxism, although it has been largely unsuccessful. When we first moved to Mainland China, it was surprising that after almost 50 years of living under Marxism, most Chinese still lived in poverty. But what was even more remarkable was that there were a few who lived in opulent luxury. Marxism had not produced a good standard of living for the masses nor had it produced equality.

One of the early steps Marxists use to reach their utopian goal is to divide people into various groups—each group falling into one of two categories, the oppressor or the oppressed. It's a very simplistic view of life. Marxism views people not as individuals, but according to the oppressor or oppressed group they have been assigned to. This means that not only is everyone in an oppressed (victim) group innocent, but everyone in an oppressor group is guilty of the alleged oppression merely because they belong to that class, regardless of their individual attitudes or actions. For example, in China, the Marxists set out to destroy everyone who had been a landlord—the landlord class—including landlords who had been kind and generous to their tenants.

This way of thinking is used to condemn, persecute, or eliminate whatever group the Marxists deem to be an obstacle to achieving their goal.[45] But in the process it produces a lot of anger and animosity between people groups, breaking down society. This enables the Marxists to divide and conquer.

Some of my older Chinese friends had suffered greatly because of

---

[45] The startling thing is that the group targeted kept changing in communist China. The early groups to be condemned, persecuted, or eliminated were those of the Nationalist Party (the non-Communist Party), anyone who had been associated with Westerners, those who owned the means of production, anyone who privately owned anything, and capitalists. After that they persecuted those who were creative or intellectual, such as artists, writers, teachers, and doctors. After all those targets had been neutralized, eventually those who were faithful believers and enforcers of Marxism were not even exempt—Red Guards and staunch Communists, whether common people or government officials, were also persecuted or killed when those with the most power came to view them as a threat. No one was safe in a Marxist state. It became apparent that the actual goal was the consolidation of the power of the elites, not the Marxist goal of equal distribution.

the oppressor class they had been assigned to, and some other older people I knew had helped to persecute or eliminate those of the oppressor classes.

§§§

Marxists like to claim that they are the solution to society's problems and inequities. But, throughout the world, it is Christians, living out their faith, who have greatly helped society's problems by building schools, hospitals, and orphanages; by taking care of and feeding the poor and disenfranchised; by raising the status of women through women's education and job opportunities; and by reducing the infant mortality rate. We saw this in China, as a number of these institutions had been established by Christian missionaries before the Chinese Communist Revolution.

§§§

Much of the core message of Marxism is contrary to the gospel message and is an assault on the gospel. First, Marxism considers that not everyone has sinned—only those they identify as oppressors have done anything wrong; the oppressed are pure. But God says that all have sinned (Romans 3:23). When I lived in Mainland China, it always struck me that one of the fatal flaws of Marxism was the assumption that the oppressed masses are good to the core, so they would be glad to share everything equally. That simply isn't true. It's the Bible's assertion that everyone is sinful and self-centered that fits reality.

Another way that Marxism is contrary to the gospel is that Marxism defines what sin is—belonging to an oppressor class or opposing Marxism. But only God can define sin because he is our creator.

In contrast to how Marxists exonerate or condemn people based on their class or ancestral heritage,[46] as far as salvation is concerned, the Lord looks at us individually. There are so many examples of this in the Old Testament. Abraham's father and family were idol worshippers

[46] There is an exception to this. If a person in a Marxist country does or says anything against the Marxist tenets, they are subject to punishment or elimination.

(Joshua 24:2-3), but Abraham believed in the true God, so he was set apart as righteous (Genesis 15:6). Rahab's people, the people of Jericho, were wicked, but God did not condemn Rahab with her people; instead, because she demonstrated faith in God, he saved her (Joshua 2). The whole chapter of Ezekiel 18 is devoted to making clear that a person is not condemned for his father's and ancestors' sin, but only for his own sin. In the New Testament we also see that we are saved as individuals, not as groups (John 3:16; Revelation 20:12-15).

Finally, the guilt assigned to the oppressor class grinds them into the dirt because there is no way to get rid of their condemnation. No amount of repentance or good deeds will absolve the "oppressors" of the stain on their souls. It's just like the worldly sorrow that brings death talked about in II Corinthians 7:10. But in contrast to Marxism offering no hope or forgiveness, Jesus offers both hope and forgiveness to everyone who believes through his sacrifice on the cross.

The fact that God deals with us individually based on our faith and actions and offers forgiveness through Jesus Christ has a lot of positive results that Marxism does not produce. In addition to being able to be forgiven and become free of guilt and condemnation (Colossians 1:22; Romans 8:1), we have motivation to change, and walk in righteousness and love because our personal actions do matter.

§§§

Another aspect of Christianity that became so beautiful to me when I encountered Marxism is our oneness in Christ. *This* is our primary identity, not our class. Galatians 3:28 makes this clear: "There is neither Jew nor Gentile, neither slave nor free, nor is there male and female, for you are all one in Christ Jesus." Our oneness in Jesus produces unity and love, not the division and animosity of Marxism.

§§§

In China I was told that prior to the Chinese Communist Revolution some Chinese Christians mistook Marxism for true Christianity. This was because on the surface Marxism's attempt to equally distribute resources can sound like Christian love.

It's interesting that Jesus himself was offered the opportunity to be the Marxist institutional answer to equal food distribution. After he fed the people bread and fish using his power, the crowd chased him down to try to make him their king so he would keep feeding the people. But he refused. (See John 6.)

When Justin taught the book of Acts during house church leader training, the leaders wanted to discuss Acts 4:32: "All the believers were one in heart and mind. No one claimed that any of their possessions was their own, but they shared everything they had." This verse has been used to defend the idea that Marxism and Christianity are the same. The house church leaders saw clearly that Acts 4:32 is an example of the early Christians lovingly living out their faith by *voluntarily* giving of what they *privately owned* to help those in need. In fact, Acts 5:4 defends private ownership where Peter states that the money from the sale of property could be used however the owner saw fit. This is completely different from Marxism, which prohibits private property and uses the *government* to force the distribution of goods. The similarity is superficial.

In fact, during our time living in China, it became apparent that Marxism in practice did not actually result in caring for the poor and disenfranchised. Instead, in China it was a system used by the elite to grab power, control, and money. The elite didn't seem to actually believe in Marxism, instead they were using its divisive message of hatred for groups of people as a way to concentrate their power.

The current leanings in America remind not only me, but also the Mainland Chinese immigrants I know in America, of the Marxist thinking we all lived under in China, with its attempt to divide people into oppressor/victim groups, to produce animosity between these groups, and to concentrate power in the hands of an elite group.

Marxism is not only completely different from Christianity, it is a direct assault on the gospel in several ways, including: who defines sin, who has sinned, and what the solution for sin is. All the fundamentals are different. It's not Marxism that liberates us, but the gospel that sets us free through repentance and faith in Jesus Christ. And it is the Lord who teaches us to love and help the poor and disenfranchised as we live out our faith. Furthermore, our unity in Christ is in stark contrast to the divisiveness of Marxism.

In a way, Marxism prepared the hearts of my Mainland Chinese friends to receive the gospel. Marxism is spiritually empty, and it only tries to supply the *material* needs of the masses. Furthermore, later during our time in Mainland China, most of the Chinese people we knew didn't believe in Marxism anymore—they were disillusioned with it, and this produced an even greater spiritual vacuum. The Lord used this spiritual vacuum, and as a result many of them became receptive to the satisfying message of Christ. That was one of the reasons why I was able to be so effective in leading Mainland Chinese people to Christ.

A GOD BEYOND COMPARISON

Observations and Conclusions

Psalm 135:18 says that people become like the gods or idols they worship. "Those who make them will be like them, and so will all who trust in them."

During my time in Asia I found that the people I knew really did become like whatever god they worshipped or whatever belief system they followed.

The idol worshippers tended to be more mercenary in their approach to life, living by quid pro quo, fundamentally self-centered, and not so concerned with morality, much like their idols.

In a moment of transparency one of my orthodox Buddhist friends told me, "Buddhists often use people, bargaining for their own benefit, because that's the way Buddhism is." And it struck me how judgmental Buddhists were, how they were constantly thinking about how other people would be punished for their bad karma. They had become like their belief system, with its great celestial scale of unrelenting justice.

Those who are deeply influenced by Marxism love power, and they seem to actually enjoy being cruel and dismissive to those who get in the way of their goals or don't agree with them. They are imitating

Marxism.

Yet there are more subtle, but important aspects of a person becoming like the god/God they worship, especially among Christians. If a Christian has a misconception about the true God, his attitudes and actions will reflect that misconception.

For example, Christians whose God is *only* law-oriented and *only* concerned with ferreting out people's shortcomings will constantly try to find the failings in those around them. They don't emphasize love, mercy, and grace, because in their thinking God is not loving, merciful, and full of grace. They have become like their misconception of God.

Christians who believe that God's *only* characteristic is that he is all loving—that he doesn't judge or get angry at wrongdoing—those Christians are usually without discernment. They are like their misconception of God, and they freely allow evil to flourish in their midst, to the detriment of everyone else.

And Christians who believe that God *only* thinks of human beings as bad and sinful, without counterbalancing that with how much the Lord delights in us and how much value Scripture shows we have—those Christians seem to devalue others. Yet the evidence in the Bible is so clear. Genesis 1:31; Zephaniah 3:17; Psalm 18:19; 147:11; and Proverbs 8:30-31 speak of how much God delights in us. And our value is evidenced by the fact that he made us in his image, and he considered us so precious that he gave his only Son to die for us.

You can often tell the aberrations in a Christian's beliefs or their view of God by their attitudes, especially toward other people.

I have noticed something that can skew a Christian's view of the true God, and that is when they hold so tightly to a particular theology that they crowbar Scripture to fit that theology. In order to have an accurate view of God, it's vital to let our beliefs and theology be formed by Scripture, and when the two clash, to let the Bible challenge and upend our theology, not the other way around.[47]

There's a human tendency to try to simplify God. The Christian God is a little wild, he is beyond what we could imagine, and he doesn't

---

[47] It's evident from Job 42:7 that when we hold a wrong view of God it can displease or anger him, even if we are holding that view to try to maintain God's honor, as Job's friends were.

fit into a box. What we see in Scripture is a multi-faceted God and a multi-faceted view of life.

I spend a lot of time soaking in the Scriptures because I yearn to know God and I want my view of him to align with who he has revealed himself to be. When I find a passage I don't like, instead of glossing over it or skipping it as I'm tempted to do, I spend *more* time on it because clearly something is wrong—I don't really understand the passage, my view of God needs adjusting, or there's a problem with my approach to life or my theology. Some of my greatest revelations about who God truly is have come from struggling with Scripture passages that irritate me, don't make sense to me, or don't fit my theology. Because I allow the Scriptures to challenge me, my faith keeps growing, and I find that God and Christianity are absolutely fascinating. There is nothing boring about God.

A true knowledge of God is foundational for us to draw near to him, and since we become like the God we worship, it is essential that we have an accurate understanding of who God really is. In addition, this is crucial to our witness to unbelievers because when the God we are sharing with unbelievers is the true God of the Bible, not just a misconception, our witness about the Lord is so much more powerful and effective.

§§§

What a beautiful faith we have! I didn't fully realize how unique and amazing our God is, and how liberating the gospel is, until I encountered other gods and beliefs while living in Hong Kong and Mainland China. You can't just add Jesus and his death on the cross to some other god and come out with the Christian God because the one true God is fundamentally different from the gods of the world. The gods people worship are not "just different parts of the same animal," as the illustration of the elephant asserts.

I worship this true God with so much more passion and abandon as a result of seeing his character in comparison to the gods and beliefs in the world.

Of course, you don't believe in a god just because he has beautiful characteristics and you're attracted to him—it's important that he actually does exist, and there is good evidence for the existence of the Christian God. But if I *were* to choose to believe in a god solely on the basis of how good he is, I would definitely choose the Christian God.

And is it any wonder that the Christian God was so appealing to the people of Hong Kong and China when they saw what he's really like in contrast to their gods?

You are very important to the success
of *Faith Ride*.

If you enjoyed the book,
please tell your friends,
write an Amazon review,
and post it on your favorite social media.

Thank you so much.

I would also love to hear from you at:
hisfragrancespreader@gmail.com

ACKNOWLEDGEMENTS

My thanks go, first of all, to Justin, my husband and my friend. He supports and makes possible my ministries, including my writing. I hope I am as much the woman behind the man as he is the man behind the woman.

I am thankful to my beta readers, especially Sam and Suzette Speights, who gave essential criticisms and encouraged me to have *Faith Ride* published.

Dr. Kevin Haley, who is the author of the awesome book, *The Egg Revealed: How Chickens Make Eggs*, made many invaluable contributions.

And special thanks to my editor, Jerri Menges, for her positive contributions.

Made in United States
Troutdale, OR
01/29/2024

17229394R00157